ESSENTIAL TOOLS FOR ORGANIZATIONAL PERFORMANCE

ESSENTIAL
TOOLS FOR
ORGANIZATIONAL
PERFORMANCE

Tools, Models and Approaches for Managers and Consultants

Simon A. Burtonshaw-Gunn
and
Malik G. Salameh

A John Wiley & Sons, Ltd., Publication

This edition first published 2009
© 2009 John Wiley & Sons, Ltd

Registered office
John Wiley & Sons Ltd, The Atrium, Southern Gate, Chichester, West Sussex,
PO19 8SQ, United Kingdom

For details of our global editorial offices, for customer services and for
information about how to apply for permission to reuse the copyright material
in this book please see our website at www.wiley.com.

Library of Congress Cataloging-in-Publication Data

Burtonshaw-Gunn, Simon A.
    Essential tools for organizational performance : tools, models and
approaches for managers and consultants / Simon A. Burtonshaw-Gunn and
Malik G. Salameh.
        p.   cm.
    Includes bibliographical references and index.
    ISBN 978-0-470-74665-3 (cloth : alk. paper)   1. Organizational change.
2. Knowledge management.   I. Salameh, Malik G.   II. Title.
    HD58.8.B8837 2009
    658.4'06—dc22

                                                            2009015947

A catalogue record for this book is available from the British Library.

Set in 11.5/15pt Bembo by SNP Best-set Typesetter Ltd., Hong Kong
Printed in Great Britain by TJ International Ltd, Padstow, Cornwall, UK

CONTENTS

ACKNOWLEDGEMENTS

Having received positive feedback on the publication of the book *The Essential Management Toolbox*, which offered a collection of models and tools that may be used for a variety of management assignments, the compilation of this sibling book would not have been possible without the fine efforts from all those management authors, research publications and course notes that we have collected over the years to inform and challenge the development of practical approaches to the topics discussed here. While we have drawn on our own writings and experience, we remain naturally still indebted to all those whose work appears in this book, and also to our own teachers and mentors who have aided our understanding on many management topics.

We are grateful to the publishers, individuals and copyright holders who gave their permission to allow previously published work to be used in this book, and while every effort has been made to ascertain copyright and seek permission we apologize in advance for any omissions and would be pleased to correct these in any future edition.

Finally, our huge thanks to all at John Wiley and Sons for their support, encouragement and the opportunity to develop the "Management Toolbox" contents in this way.

ABOUT THE AUTHORS

Professor Simon A. Burtonshaw-Gunn has over 30 years' working experience in both the public and private sectors covering a range of organizations and industries. As a practising management consultant he has undertaken assignments in Asia, North Africa, the Middle and Far East and Eastern Europe, and currently holds a full-time position as a Principal Management Consultant for the international risk management consultancy company, Risktec Solutions Limited. In addition, he has a *pro bono* position as a member of the Court at the University of Leeds – a member of the Russell Group Association of the top 20 UK research-intensive universities. To complement this experience he holds two Master's degrees and a PhD in various strategic management topics together with fellowships of four professional bodies including the Chartered Management Institute (FCMI) and the Institute of Business Consulting (FIBC).

He was a post-doctoral research fellow for four years at the Manchester Metropolitan University before relinquishing this at the beginning of 2005 to take up the role of a visiting professor at the University of Salford in Greater Manchester. Here he served for three years in the six-star research rated School of the Built Environment before being appointed as the first visiting professor to the Salford Business School in 2007. Professor Burtonshaw-Gunn has been a research examiner for the UK's Chartered Institute of Purchasing and Supply (CIPS) since 2002 and is one of the founding members of an international academic research group (ISCRiM) with a focus on supply chain risk management. In connection with this group he has presented conference papers in Sweden, the USA, the UK and Hungary together with a number of refereed publications, professional journal articles and chapters in four collaborative management textbooks. On the subject of risk management he has recently published a book covering "Risk and Financial Management in Construction" aimed at industry practitioners and post-graduate students. His popular book *The Essential Management Toolbox*, covering management tools, models and notes aimed at students, managers and consultants alike, was published by John Wiley and Sons in January 2008.

Dr Malik G. Salameh read Aeronautical Engineering for his first degree, before completing a Master's degree in Business and Operations Management and then specializing in implementing value-based cultural change within "blue-chip" corporate environments. He holds a PhD in Management and is an active member of a number of professional bodies including the Royal

Aeronautical Society (MRAeS), the Chartered Institute of Marketing (MCIM), the Chartered Management Institute (MCMI) and the Chartered Institute of Personnel and Development (MCIPD).

Dr Salameh is a practising management consultant undertaking a wide range of strategic consultancy assignments in the UK and internationally including the Middle and Far East, North Africa, Eastern Europe, North America and Asia. His focus includes supporting senior management teams in all aspects of organizational design and development through to transition and implementation at both tactical and strategic levels. He actively contributes to the continued development of his discipline through publications, attendance at CPD lectures, debates and master classes at Lancaster University Management School, which is among the top MBA schools in the world and the first to be awarded a six star rating in the UK. He has also been selected as post-doctoral examiner for Warwick University Business School in the UK.

Professor Burtonshaw-Gunn and Dr Salameh have undertaken a range of management consultancy assignments together both in the UK and in more challenging international locations where skills, experience and academic knowledge require a wider cultural appreciation, understanding and respect of the external economic, political, religious and business influences. Over the last four years they have published a number of joint articles on a range of business topics with an established house style of combining management theory with practical experience.

INTRODUCTION

This book has been developed from an interest in the use of management tools and models published in January 2008 in *The Essential Management Toolbox: Tools, Models and Notes for Managers and Consultants*. This supplementary book describes a number of examples and shares the authors' practical experiences in the use of appropriate management tools and models taken from the Toolbox with a focus on the topic of organizational development and performance.

As an introduction, this book comprises five broad and inter-related chapters commencing with Process Management, leading to Change Management and Organizational Development, then to People-focused Performance Management and the role of Knowledge Management applicable to organizational and individual performance. The final chapter examines the topic of organizational development and performance from closer collaborative-partnered work between organizations.

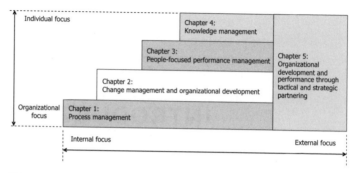

Figure 0.1 Development of performance management.

These chapters also present a balance between the organizations and individual performance commitment, although clearly both are needed to a greater or lesser extent in each topic.

It should be noted that the book title reflects that the narrative describes a range of tools and models on this important management topic and that the five chapters may be viewed as standalone topics or as elements of a systematic approach to organizational development and performance management. However, in practice, of course, the five topics will not always be applicable to every company.

The book is designed to be one of a series of sibling publications intended to group enabling management tools, techniques and models into related clusters. These publications will give managers, organizational leaders and consultancy practitioners a highly effective means of developing a composite view of an organization and where necessary helping to apply an appropriate level of intervention to drive performance improvement. Other titles are *Essential Tools for Management Consulting* and *Essential Tools for Operations Management.*

The structure follows the successful Toolbox formula of integrating contemporary management tools, techniques and models with those developed from practical experience of addressing the interconnectedness of a wide range of organizational challenges across multiple industries. While this approach provides the opportunity to discuss some new models, the majority of the figures and models are taken from *The Essential Management Toolbox: Tools, Models and Notes for Managers and Consultants.* Where the original source is not that of the authors then the source is shown with each model discussed. As with *The Essential Management Toolbox* and other books in this series, full references are provided to guide the reader to where further information may be found. To assist the reader, each chapter is punctuated by key theme subheadings to aid navigation and provide a logical approach to each topic area together with accompanying explanations intended to facilitate robust analysis, gain commitment and develop momentum.

The intent of writing this title has been again to provide a suitable reference for those currently studying, newly qualified or promoted managers or those business leaders wishing to understand and undertake practical performance improvements relevant to the latest management thinking. The incremental nature of the book content is planned to act as a catalyst in reducing the lead-time to developing practical responses to changes in market dynamics and assist the application of right-sizing throughout any organization's development lifecycle, with an equal relevance to both the public and private sectors. It should be noted that both "hard" and "soft" management issues are balanced to help emphasize the importance of symbiotic relationships in engaging people, achieving high performance and driving innovation through active knowledge management, all of which has been covered in this text. Finally, the use of the plan–do–review theme is deliberate throughout the book to allow any manager, facilitator or change agent to deliver performance improvement in a structured and effective format.

CHAPTER 1

PROCESS IMPROVEMENT

DEVELOPMENTS IN PROCESS MANAGEMENT

Businesses, whether commercial or not-for-profit organizations, inevitably have a wish to remain in operation; to have sustainable and repeatable business; and to satisfy stakeholders, customers and employees. For many, this brings a need to examine their operations in order to improve and advance such objectives. While organization change is covered in detail in Chapter 2 and the people aspects of performance management and organizational development in Chapter 3, a deliberate starting point for such change may be the examination of current practices and processes. Against this backdrop, process improvement can be regarded as being a systematic effort to provide an understanding of every aspect of a company's processes in order to reduce rework, variation and needless complexity in order to contribute to its performance through effectiveness and efficiency. It should be noted that process identification and redesign only provides a benefit when it is actually implemented and hence this also suggests a natural link to a change management programme.

Completion of a process improvement examination exercise is often seen to be a traditional springboard for much larger business improvements, which may in turn incrementally develop into a large-scale change management programme and planned organizational development. Indeed, what may begin as a simple local business improvement may grow into other initiatives aimed at delivering more substantial change and hence increased business-wide implications. The evolution through a range of such business programmes is shown in Figure 1.1.

With every organizational change there comes a risk which usually manifests itself through deterioration in business performance; however, a performance management system with associated key performance indicators can be used to help management teams predict and mitigate such an impact. This suggests that process improvement may be made in conjunction with the introduction of a change management programme which may be instigated

Figure 1.1 The re-engineering spectrum.
(From *Business Process Re-engineering: Myth and Reality*. Professor Colin Coulson-Thomas, 1996, reproduced with permission of Kogan Page.)

to realign the culture and business targets. Nevertheless, it should be stressed that the ubiquity of change management initiatives within both public and private sector organizations can quite often leave stakeholders at all levels with "change fatigue", particularly where the vision, mission and principal objectives become diluted and performance reporting data confused. This said, for any performance-based management system to really add value to the organization it will need to encourage a no-blame culture where it will be safe for individuals to highlight sources of poor performance variance and actually regard these as proactive opportunities for improvement through a step change in their process redesign activities prior to implementation. Common across the re-engineering spectrum of Figure 1.1 is the requirement to understand

Revolution	Evolution
BPR – Business Process Re-engineering	Continuous improvement
Start from scratch	Kaizen
Very rapid	Build on what has gone before
Innovative	Slowly and steady
	Maintenance and improvement

Figure 1.2   Two extremes of undertaking process improvement. (From *The Essential Management Toolbox: Tools, Models and Notes for Managers and Consultants*. S.A. Burtonshaw-Gunn, 2008, reproduced with permission.)

fully the current processes together with a desire to improve them.

Consequently, it is essential that organizations establish a level of openness and engagement throughout the process improvement and change management lifecycle, which transcends policies, procedures and statutory obligations, and carefully consider how critical the involvement of all employees will be in helping deliver process change. While there are a number of approaches to change, there are two extremes of major step change – one being revolution and the other a more gentle, incremental change of evolution with the features of both shown in Figure 1.2. However, this is not to suggest that one of these types is good and the other poor as this choice depends on a range of circumstances and the host organization's drivers for change. It should also be noted that a combination of these approaches is also possible although the majority of process improvements are aimed at achieving significant operational and financial improvement; as such, the revolution elements of a business process re-engineering approach such as process mapping are commonly adopted.

In considering the other extreme category of process improvement, the term evolution is aptly used as this supports a continual activity. Without such commitment, it is likely that the company's performance will fail to keep pace with its competitors and larger change will more likely then be required. This failure is commonly referred to as "strategic drift" and is also shown in the model of Figure 2.2 in Chapter 2.

INVESTIGATING BUSINESS PROCESSES

While the obvious starting point is to gain an understanding and evaluation of an organization's current processes in order to identify where waste and/or rework occurs, it is also possible to take a more "visionary" approach and look to producing new processes without the constraints or inhibitions imposed by an organization's current operations and capability. This Envision stage exists in the standard business process re-engineering (BPR) methodology and requires an identification of any gaps to be undertaken and quantified in order to identify the level of transition to made to the "to-be" processes of the organization compared with those of the organization's current "as-is" position. A widely employed approach to BPR is shown in Figure 1.3. As mentioned above, the

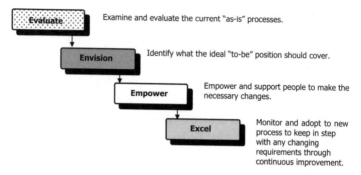

Figure 1.3 Business improvement process.
(From *The Essential Management Toolbox: Tools, Models and Notes for Managers and Consultants*. S.A. Burtonshaw-Gunn, 2008, reproduced with permission.)

starting point on the model may be either at the Evaluate or Envision stage, although both stages will need to be ultimately addressed.

One of the well-known and commonly used models in Europe is the EFQM Business Excellence model (covered as Figure 3.2 in Chapter 3), which itself has similarities to the American "Malcolm Baldrige National Quality Award", both of which prompt organizations to look at their processes and in particular question how they are developed, used, reviewed and updated. At a higher level the Business Excellence model also promotes the use of "best practice" benchmarking with other companies and places great emphasis on performance measurement over time allowing trend analysis to be undertaken. This performance measurement can be from qualitative data from customer or employee feedback, or from quantitative data such as financial reports, defect rates, etc. and used to examine the alignment relationship of the company processes to its business and customer requirements.

Since the mid 1950s, process examination has been part of the topic of "work study", itself a forerunner to industrial engineering and more latterly management systems. As part of the earlier industrial tools, work study was a systematic approach of a staged methodology to select, record, examine, develop, install and maintain processes with the objective of reducing waste and hence increasing industrial output and performance.

One of the models that can be used to compare and contrast similar processes in an organization, especially if these are undertaken at different locations, is the POLDAT approach first used by the American Computer Services Corporation, and shown as Figure 1.4. This is used to record:

- the processes undertaken;
- the organizational setting;
- the location of where the processes are undertaken;
- the data that are managed;
- the application of the data; and finally
- the technology used in undertaking the task.

In addition to this internal comparison is the growing use of "benchmarking" where comparison is made with similar industries and companies to mutually seek

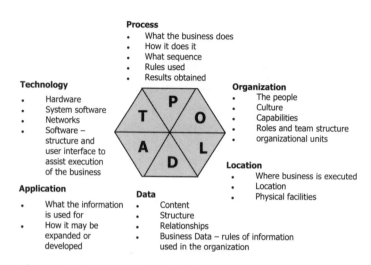

Figure 1.4   POLDAT methodology.
(From *The Essential Management Toolbox: Tools, Models and Notes for Managers and Consultants*. S.A. Burtonshaw-Gunn, 2008, reproduced with permission.)

improvement in process operations and share examples of considered good practice.

The use of the POLDAT model provides a systematic approach to selecting and recording performance whether at the company, department or activity level and lends itself to being a basis of comparison with the same activities undertaken in different locations. Such a comparison prompts questions around the model components such as details of the process; the organization's resources in terms of roles, responsibilities and numbers; and the use, level and extent of technology involved in undertaking each activity, etc. in order to perform the same work output. Where process improvement is sought across a wide geographical area, companies can often address process improvement through the establishment of virtual teams and external consultant input, or at the other extreme have their own full-time staff charged with undertaking process improvement activity across an organization. The later is more commonly used in the larger international organizations where the internal cost of establishing and operating such a team is more easily absorbed by the business. For some companies process improvement may also arise from other business activities such as problem solving.

One of the most used tools in this area is process mapping which encourages detailed investigation and analysis of how the company discharges its work. Process maps are usually presented in the form of a flow diagram and often have their own drawing convention. While flow charts may be drawn in a common IT program such as Microsoft Powerpoint or Excel, there are a number of process-mapping software programs such as Visio, FlowCharter Plus and Process Expert Professional, the latter being favoured by some UK police forces, for example. When considering the process language there are a number of mapping conventions such as British Standards, ASME Standard for Process Charts, etc. In widespread use is the internationally recognized Unified Modelling Language. However, the choice of these is of little consequence as it is the *task of process mapping* itself that provides an understanding of the current processes that can later be developed into new processes aimed at providing real performance benefits. If the process cannot be drawn using these mapping symbols then it is suggested that the process itself is not sufficiently understood. In view of the timing – or, perhaps more accurately, the order – of such an investigation the starting points of Evaluate or Envision shown in the business improvement process in Figure 1.3 again suggest either of these two stages provides an appropriate starting point providing that this is supported by the organization and those requesting an analysis of the organization's processes and performance.

Process improvement can also draw heavily on benchmarking an organization's processes with those of other businesses, although in practice finding "best practice" examples is not always easy, and often some examples are difficult to transfer between companies due to cultural or other operational differences. This is not to suggest that benchmarking is of no value, but that the elements of best practice championed by one organization may not always be applicable to others. It should also be noted that closer collaborative working (see Chapter 5) can also provide useful insights into process performance improvements where instead of whole process transfers, smaller "nuggets" of best practice may be identified which can be incorporated into providing increased organizational performance. The following six-step approach to benchmarking is proposed:

1. Define which process or practice is to be benchmarked and what you currently do.
2. Identify any best practice award winners in the area you wish to benchmark and list contact persons who could be potential partners.
3. Select and approach benchmark partners and explain the potential benefits to both sides.
4. Conduct one or more benchmark visits, identify learning points and provide feedback to the benchmark partner.
5. Use the learning points to create a benchmark report and options.
6. Agree the next steps and trial implementation improvements.

RECORDING THE PROCESSES

In almost all cases, irrespective of the starting position, a typical process improvement investigation will follow the process mapping to show the sequence of activities, flow of information, decision points and the range of possible process outcomes.

While simple process mapping provides a logical sequential account of the activities under investigation, this may be further refined by mapping the activities to align with individual roles or groups of staff and thus provide an organizational linkage between the process activities and the HR structure. The most common method of this linkage is by producing process maps arranged in "swim-lanes" headed by the appropriate resource grouping or individual post-holders. This method also allows the identification of those who should be involved in the current (as-is) process mapping together with identifying organizational changes on development of the "to-be" process maps. Again, the swim-lane approach provides a relatively easy method to understand the contribution made by groups (or individuals), which can then be cross-referenced with the existing or new role/job descriptions. The lanes can be punctuated with stage markers similar to those used in a swimming pool, providing an easy indication for the process user of which part of the process they are involved in and the following major stages to be undertaken. In addition, it is suggested that it is also beneficial to note the objectives of the process at the start of the map as this sets the scene for the user and provides some confidence that it is being undertaken for a specific and identified business purpose. Performance improvements can be made by building on the process mapping work – not just in modifying exist-ing processes or introducing new ones, but by removing duplicated work or introducing changes to provide a closer synergy between related process maps. Looking at the roles and responsibilities of the staff undertaking the processes provides opportunities to improve further per-formance requirements including resource management and succession planning necessary to maintain operational performance or indeed required regulatory compliance in some industries. From an HRM or staff training perspective, process mapping also supports a clear understanding of the business processes for employees new to an organization or department. Bearing this in mind from a more strategic viewpoint, process mapping, its development and adherence should be linked to wider quality assurance company requirements where applicable.

The final two models of this first chapter (Figures 1.5 and 1.6) each present an opportunity to examine the resulting processes maps and identify further improvements. First, Figure 1.5 provides not only a step-by-step list for process mapping but offers much more than simply stating what is done by, more importantly, prompting the complier to examine the tasks further by the addition of some guidance questions which can be asked at each of the seven steps. This was first published by Christopher Ahoy of Iowa State University and is reproduced below with his permission.

The table of Figure 1.6 provides some further practical prompts to those tasked with seeking process improvements and is a useful tool to use following on from Chris Ahoy's model. The questions of Figure 1.6 can be used both by an individual process mapper and by a group in a workshop environment to facilitate further process improvement following an examination of the "as-is" process maps and the development of the new "to-be" process improvements. The primary questions are initially designed to check that all of the required information has been obtained; after which the next stage is to enquire

Step 1: Determine the boundaries	• Where does a process begin? • Where does a process end?
Step 2: List the steps	• Use a verb to start the task description. • The flowchart can either show the sufficient information to understand the general process flow or detail every finite action and decision point.
Step 3: Sequence the steps	• Use post-it notes so you can move tasks. • Do not draw arrows until later.
Step 4: Draw appropriate symbols	Start with the basic symbols: • Ovals show input to start the process or output at the end of the process. • Boxes or rectangles show task or activity performed in the process. • Arrows show process direction flow. • Diamonds show points in the process where yes/no questions are asked or a decision is required. • Usually there is only one arrow out of an activity box. If there is more than one arrow, you may need a decision diamond. If there are feedback arrows, make sure feedback loop is closed, i.e. it should take you back to the input box.
Step 5: System model	• Draw charts using system model approach. • Input – use information based upon people, machines, material, method and environment. • Process – use subsets of processes in series or parallel. • Output – use outcomes or desired results. • Control – use best in class business rules. • Feedback – use information from surveys or feedback.
Step 6: Check for completeness	• Include pertinent chart information, using title and date for easy reference.
Step 7: Finalize the flowchart	• Ask if this process is being run the way it should be. • Are people following the process as charted? • Is there a consensus? • What is redundant; add what is missing.

Figure 1.5 Process mapping.
(From *Process Mapping, Facilities Planning and Management.* C. Ahoy, 1999, reproduced with permission of Iowa State University.)

why the identified process steps are undertaken, their sequence and the organizational benefits from undertaking them. However, greater value may be obtained as a result of addressing the secondary questions as it is these

PRIMARY QUESTIONS	WHY?	SECONDARY QUESTIONS	SELECTION
PURPOSE – What is achieved?	WHY?	What else could be achieved?	WHAT SHOULD be achieved?
MEANS – How is it achieved?	WHY THAT WAY?	How else could it be achieved?	HOW SHOULD it be achieved?
SEQUENCE – When is it achieved?	WHY THEN?	When could it be achieved?	WHEN SHOULD it be achieved?
PLACE – Where is it achieved?	WHY THERE?	Where else could it be achieved?	WHERE SHOULD it be achieved?
PERSON – Who achieves it?	WHY THAT PERSON?	Who else could achieve it?	WHO SHOULD achieve it?

Figure 1.6   Process map development.

that initiate deeper investigation of the proposed "to-be" process and ultimately contribute to achieving improved performance.

Such questioning should also suggest that the process developer considers the implications of *not* doing parts of the process and the external impact on the organization's current or potential customers or stakeholders. The items that need to change can be captured and used as part of the change management process. Options on this topic are provided in the next chapter.

CHANGE MANAGEMENT AND ORGANIZATIONAL DEVELOPMENT

DEVELOPMENTS IN CHANGE MANAGEMENT

When considering the drivers for organizational change it has to be said that nothing remains still in the world of business. The rate of change that companies face has continued at an increasing pace over the last 50 years through advances in technology since the 1960s and more recently through the globalization of supply chains. While historically change did occur this was generally focused on alignment with customer demand and technological advances in production techniques and was usually addressed by incrementally stepped change. As the rate of change increased so the gap widened between global competitors necessitating more extensive change management plans and longer implementation lead-times. Such planned major change is often an infrequent action and part of a larger organizational realignment either through incremental drift of lagging behind others or the need for a more large-scale change driven by evolution or revolution.

All organizations are destined therefore either to perish through business failure from being left behind by the competition or to accept that undertaking change is a natural part of business life in order to keep in line with the need for improvements or customer or fashion demands. Even where organizations are engaged in their own change derived from incremental improvements this can often be behind that demanded by the changes in the business environment resulting in further action being needed to gain closer realignment. The model in Figure 2.1 shows that the business environment changes at a pace faster than the organization's change strategy, which over time fails to develop in line with it. In reality, it is often difficult to ensure that the organization remains aligned with external influences as each subtle change can be undetected on its own; however, many organizations will recognize the reality shown in Figure 2.1 and the need to be aware of the relative additional external changes.

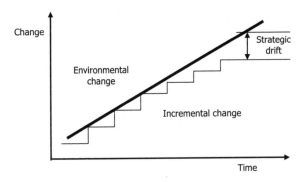

Figure 2.1 Strategic drift and trigger for change.
(From *Management Concepts and Practices*. Dr Tim Hannagan, 2005, reproduced with permission of Pearson Education.)

While this chapter provides a number of models about managing change, it is stressed that even accounting for the strategic drift any change management plan is destined to fail unless supported by a main sponsor. It is considered that this should be the senior management of the organization in place of the organization's stakeholders who must also have an acceptance that such change is seen as being appropriate for the specific organization and that its customer base will respond positively to the changes as and when they are implemented.

Even with senior management support, the change process is likely to be time consuming and the company will have to consider the type of change strategy best suited to pursue the organization's new direction. There are a number of factors that will need to be considered in choosing how to implement the necessary

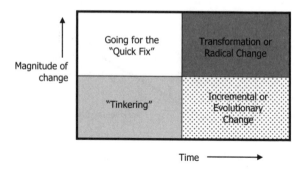

Figure 2.2 Change options.
(From *The Essential Management Toolbox: Tools, Models and Notes for Managers and Consultants*. S.A. Burtonshaw-Gunn, 2008, reproduced with permission.)

changes as each approach will be appropriate to different circumstances. Indeed, it is stressed that those that are inconsistent with the demands of the situation – the people, the cultural setting and the business environment – will undoubtedly run into problems and fail to provide the long-term benefits of the required changes.

While there are a number of change options open to organizations, as shown in Figure 2.2, it should be noted that undertaking any specific change management programme is neither easy nor should be thought of as a quick undertaking; however, there are some models and approaches included in this chapter which may assist those considering undertaking or indeed tasked with delivering organizational change.

Recognition of the need to justify, communicate and train staff in change management to minimize resistance to proposed change not only needs to be sensitively managed, but has always been a feature of undertaking change from established practices across the ages. The advice penned by the sixteenth-century Italian courtier Nicholo Machiavelli is often quoted by those involved in undertaking this task: "There is nothing more difficult to take in hand, more perilous to conduct, or more uncertain in its success, than to take the lead in the introduction of a new order of things" (*The Prince*, published in 1532).

CHANGE MANAGEMENT CONSIDERATIONS

Bearing in mind the above historical advice and the recognition of the level of difficulty of introducing change, the model shown as Figure 2.3 shows a range of changes which an organization may wish to adopt. The model also suggests that the easier changes at the bottom of the pyramid offer the least level of discomfort for employees and that these lower level changes also require the least amount of time and cost. Similarly, the higher levels necessitate substantial time and investment and as such are much harder to implement. The pyramid model also suggests that embarking on the lower level changes first may be a good way to develop an acceptance to a change programme especially if quick, beneficial and easy to observe changes can be realized by this staged approach

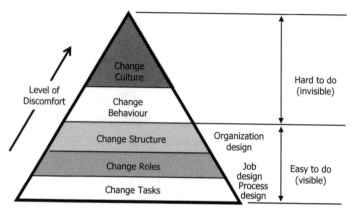

Figure 2.3   Change pyramid.
(From *The Essential Management Toolbox: Tools, Models and Notes for Managers and Consultants*. S.A. Burtonshaw-Gunn, 2008, reproduced with permission.)

– a clear example of harvesting "the low hanging fruit" first.

After considering the above factors, it is proposed that there are five broad optional approaches that can be deployed in change implementation. These may be applicable to all of the options given in the change pyramid but in practice offer maximum benefit for more major change initiatives such as those involving behaviour or cultural change. These are shown in Figure 2.4 and described in detail below.

Directive strategy: In this strategy the management can use its authority to impose the changes required and be able to carry them out speedily. However, the dis-

Figure 2.4 Strategies for change.
(From *Change Management and Organizational Performance.* S.A. Burtonshaw-Gunn and M.G. Salameh, ICAFI University Press, 2007a.)

advantage of this approach is that it is likely to increase resistance by those involved or even undermine the overall success of the change implementation.

Expert strategy: This approach is usually applied when a "technical" problem requires solving, such as the introduction of a new IT system, and as such is better suited to smaller technical or operational change than a wider cultural-change requirement. It is also appropriate that introducing technical changes does not easily lend itself to wider consultation as knowledge of the technical nuances may reside only with a limited number of individuals.

Negotiating strategy: This strategy involves a willingness to negotiate with individuals and teams affected by the change and to accept that adjustments and concessions may have to be made. Opting for this approach does not remove the management's responsibility for the direction and initiation of change but acknowledges that those affected have the right to have some input in the changes proposed, or that they have some power to resist it if they are not supportive. The advantage of selecting this approach is that resistance to the proposed change is likely to be reduced. However, such negotiation will add to the overall programme and the pre-implementation time may take longer. Changing work practices in return for increased pay and/or other benefits is a classic example of the negotiating strategy.

Educative strategy: This approach involves changing people's values and beliefs so that they support the change and are committed to a shared set of organizational values. Winning "hearts and minds" is a complex process that involves a mixture of activities such as: communication, persuasion, education, training and selection. The advantage of such an approach, if successful, is that people will be positively committed to the change. In general, this approach typically takes much longer and requires more resources than the previous three strategies described above.

Participative strategy: This strategy has a number of advantages in its implementation: changes are more likely to be widely acceptable over the other strategies; it promotes an active involvement of people and is likely to increase their commitment to, and enthusiasm for, the change process. Additionally, there will be opportunities for both managers and employees to learn from the experiences and skills of this wide participation. While this has a number of advantages due to the participation of staff, the identified changes are likely to take longer and require additional resources to support the change.

While each of these five strategies may offer a number of primary approaches, which can be matched to the factors discussed above, it is suggested that the most appropriate change strategy for organizations that need to realize new values, processes and behaviours is through the use of a participative strategy. In addition, it is further suggested that the educative strategy of communication with staff, the primary customers, stakeholders and potential new customers should also be used to augment operational changes and harmonize support.

For any identified changes to be successfully adopted, merely introducing some new pieces of equipment, or a new process, is unlikely to have any major impact on the organization unless introduced as part of an overall and coordinated change process. When considering a major change programme both technical and managerial changes are likely to be widespread and have an impact on all of the elements of the organization, as shown in Figure 2.5.

A brief explanation of the elements of the organizational model by Kelvin Hard and how each is related

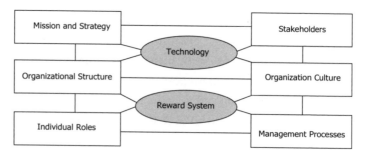

Figure 2.5 Major organizational components impacted by a change management programme.
(Source: Kelvin Hard, Developing the right organization, in *Strategies for Human Resource Management*. M. Armstrong (ed.), Kogan Page Limited, 1994.)

specifically to an organization change programme is discussed below.

- The *mission and strategy* is an important element of the organization as it provides a clear declaration of intent and serves as a reference point to establishing any required changes. While the vision, mission and its strategic objectives may have been developed, a wider communication of these with staff will prevent confusion and ambiguity over the logic behind the proposed changes and the business's long-term development plans. There is widespread evidence to show that publishing the mission statement whenever possible promotes its significance and relevance to employees' day-to-day activities, such as in meetings, or exceeds customer's expectations; fosters a managerial culture that is customer-responsive; and contributes to individual and business performance.

- The support of the *stakeholders* is important for any change plan to be successful; this should not be restricted to the owners but should include all staff, principal customers, suppliers and others who provide support to the business in its day-to-day or long-term business activities.

- An *organization's culture* is one of the major influences that makes each business different. Typically, this is witnessed in its rules on behaviour; its beliefs about what is important and good for the organization; its management style and levels of authority; and finally the corporate image of the organization as portrayed as an employer or a customer. Clearly, the introduction of changes in an organization will have a subsequent impact on modifying its present culture, particularly if the business expands into new geographic markets.

- Development of the "right" *organization structure* in support of the business plan can lead to improvements in functional responsibility and business performance. Such changes can be implemented as part of the change management plan as and when the roles and responsibilities have been defined, when the selection and appointments to any new positions have been made and when existing staff development programmes have been agreed. The introduction of a new organization structure can be very emotive and will often need careful planning. This should not be taken lightly as this will require senior management time and effort to help staff to understand their new roles and processes. Developing the organization structure may also be linked to the process mapping activities described in Chapter 1.

• The world is continually changing through business process improvements gained from the introduction of new *technology* and wider media connectivity; from a customer expectations viewpoint both of these increase the pressure on the business to perform efficiently. Any technology changes identified in a company's business plan must be seen to contribute to the main objectives, its stated mission and longer-term vision statement.

• All organizations are made up of *individual* people whose *roles* interact; as such the design of their roles is important and will be a key aspect in the organizational development of a company as it changes to embrace a new business focus. Within the context of a proposed change programme, work is often needed on new processes or new performance requirements to produce new job profiles, person specifications and requirements, and finally to undertake staff selection and consider their long-term development. Such learning and development should also focus on enhancing personnel operations to help to achieve higher standards of competence and performance.

- Depending on the company structure, some of the important *management processes* usually take place across the functional hierarchy such as planning and budgeting, systems development, succession planning, customer-related activities and management/staff development. In addition to these business processes, the importance of communication needs to be regarded as being of major importance for organizations undergoing a change programme. Indeed, for those undertaking large-scale change this should be regarded as being fundamental to preparing and implementing the identified changes in the company.

- The final element of the model of Figure 2.5 is that of *reward systems*. These are an important part of any organization's attractiveness and ability to encourage people to become and remain as its employees; to secure a level of commitment and effort; to encourage the necessary behaviour to support the organization performance targets; and finally to support flexibility, creativity and innovation as the organization develops.

CHANGE MANAGEMENT PLANNING

Having considered and selected the most appropriate change strategy and described the elements that need to be acknowledged as part of the change process with

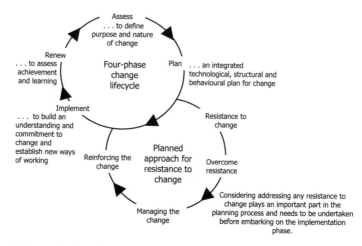

Figure 2.6   Planning organizational change.
(From *The Essential Management Toolbox: Tools, Models and Notes for Managers and Consultants.* S.A. Burtonshaw-Gunn, 2008, reproduced with permission.)

respect to individuals and the organization itself, the model of Figure 2.6 illustrates how the change programme may be implemented. In line with any quality management philosophy of "plan–do–review", implementing change is no different as it also needs to be assessed, planned, implemented and reviewed.

The model in Figure 2.6 not only illustrates the phases of the change cycle but also recognizes that resistance to change needs to be acknowledged and professionally managed.

Research suggests that for those implementing a change programme there are three inter-related skills categories which managers need to possess in order to promote effective change. These are:

1. *Transforming skills* where managers need to be able to create a supportive risk-taking environment, have self-awareness and self-confidence. They will need to possess the ability to share the benefits that the change will bring and the journey needed to undertake this through visualization techniques.
2. *Mental skills* will require managers to think holistically and help others to see the "big picture". These managers will be able to work with rules of thumb based on action learning.
3. Managers in a change environment will be required to have the "softer" skills of *empathy and understanding of feelings*. Often these will be witnessed through the use of symbols, analogies and metaphors to relate to the change process and will need the ability to tolerate stress and resist confronting every issue. These skills demand use of both left and right side brain techniques.

It should be noted that as improved performance is often a goal in undertaking a change management programme this can only be delivered by people and as such Chapter 3 seeks to share some useful models applicable to people-focused performance management. The next model of this chapter is used to describe a practical large-scale change programme where typical key activities may be undertaken in the three phases. While there will be some deviation to accommodate local business, cultural or stakeholders' requirements, this three-phase model provides a good basis for those planning change and defining a practical approach in its undertaking. This model is a practical adoption of the theory of "unfreezing, transformation and re-freezing" from Kurt Lewin's model of change developed as early as 1947. The three proposed phases are outlined in Figure 2.7 and the specific details of an actual change programme are then described below. It should also be noted that after these major changes have been implemented, smaller incremental changes will

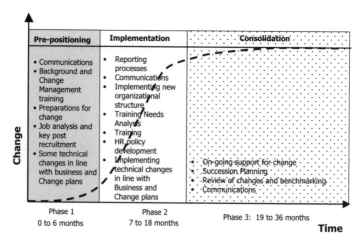

Figure 2.7 Large-scale change management aligned to phases of a programme.
(From *Change Management and Organizational Performance*. S.A. Burtonshaw-Gunn and M.G. Salameh, ICAFI University Press, 2007a.)

often follow on as part of a philosophy of not as "change management" but as continual business improvement.

Phase 1: Organizational pre-positioning: The first phase can typically be of six months' duration and should focus on the preparations for change through communications with staff and stakeholders. In addition, it can consist of some initial job analysis including preparation of job descriptions for the introduction of a new organization structure and the delivery of general change management awareness training to staff. This phase is aimed at preparing the organization for change and managing the associated risks and benefits. The main activities in this phase are described below.

Communications: A fundamental aspect of expediting a change process throughout the implementation phase will be developing an initial awareness and understanding at an early stage as to why such a change management process is required and the benefits to be gained at organizational, team and individual performance levels. Clearly, this pre-positioning work is fundamental in shaping and successfully delivering the required knowledge to take the organization from its current business mode of operation through to achieving its desired higher performing business vision. Such pre-positioning will also allow reinforcement of the key strategic messages behind the change management implementation plan and how business critical functions are an integral part of realizing an organization which is commercially attractive and transparently accountable. From practical experience, at no point throughout the communications cycle should the change management implementation timeframe be delivered in anything but the most realistic terms. If this is not the case, it can severely hinder the level of employee commitment and the credibility of the programme and transformation to be embedded.

General awareness training and analysis: The first stage of designing a focused and relevant training and learning agenda is to ensure that the activities are aimed at raising awareness of the appropriate skills and knowledge required. A training needs analysis (TNA) is usually a good starting point and can be undertaken in conjunction with a detailed cultural audit of the organization, using competency frameworks and job profiles of the identified jobs in any proposed future structure. All managers will be required to provide information on individuals, using a framework of the competencies for each job profile. In addition to information on employees, the business strategy and objectives will also determine the key areas required to deliver the planned changes and improved organizational processes. The combination of the data will provide the basis for a generic training plan, recognize individual development needs of the staff and establish a priority for delivery. The training focus early in this first phase will generally be concerned with creating an organization-wide awareness of the drivers for change, the need to adapt to a changing competitive environment and promoting the fact that the programme has strong commitment and leadership from the senior management of the organization. The programme may also need to include a foundation level customer service training and commercial awareness module for all staff to meet a defined standard and to address current levels of customer service provision.

Job analysis and organization structure preparations: At this initial phase of the change management programme, it is proposed that the organization structure will only be beginning its transition; however, integral to this will be a job analysis of the key post-holders to aid the preparations for structuring the new organization. This is an important exercise for the organization in establishing where the core knowledge and experience lies and among which key individuals or areas this is vested. If the change objective is proposing to adopt a number of new business practices and processes aimed at providing the organization with improved business performance, then conducting a job analysis across the complete spectrum of strategic organizational roles and responsibilities will also need be undertaken at the earliest opportunity. This personnel information will provide the necessary data to help structure a personal and collective performance framework in line with the organization's planned changes and future business performance goals.

HR environment: A strategic HRM approach has a very different ethos to purely the existence of a limited HR function. The key distinction is that it cannot be imposed as part of a short-term change management objective, but needs to be progressively developed as a core functional capability over a longer term; ideally focused around an experience-based learning culture. It is important that the HR function is sufficiently cohesive and achieves an appropriate level of change awareness in Phase 1, as it will be instrumental in helping both to reduce resistance to proposed changes by providing a safe learning environment and to communicate supportive messages to which it will also be committed. To promote a consistent and fair approach to organizational and functional development, there will need to be created an ongoing coordination forum with representatives from all the functions, focused on involvement in managing the HRM impacts of the wider strategic change plan. Depending on the organization, this is likely to include departments such as finance, technical services, operations, support services and business development.

Technical change implementation: It may be appropriate to introduce a number of the technical changes identified in the business and change management plans within the timescale of Phase 1. However, the majority of these technical changes are often best suited to be implemented in Phase 2 after the change management training and major communications events have pre-positioned the organization and prepared the staff to anticipate and become involved in the proposed changes.

Phase 2: Change management plan implementation: Moving to Phase 2 will cover the next 12 month period on completion of Phase 1. The focus now should be on the implementation of the changes against the agreed plans and the business objectives. During this phase, progress of the implementation should be regularly reported to the senior managers, staff and stakeholders (and shareholders if applicable). The main activities in this second phase are as follows.

Communications: During the second phase, the communications emphasis will move from preparation of the employees for change to an ongoing process of reinforcement of the corporate message and cultural values throughout the three-phase programme. One of the most effective means for doing this will be to utilize an ongoing learning and development arena, which will afford the opportunity to review all aspects of the organizational development at key critical process milestones. Additionally, this can also be fed back as part of the organizational learning and development cycle. This ongoing review cycle when linked to skills transfer activities will also allow the identification of areas where there are gaps or a perceived lack of clarity over the direction the organization is taking. It is likely that this will highlight whether there is a need for a number of ongoing communication events reporting key strategic decisions and explaining how each fits with the change management strategy.

Training design and delivery: Long-term training needs should be linked back to the initial TNA undertaken as part of Phase 1 work. Once the data have been analysed, suitable programmes can then be designed for all staff. This is likely to cover a variety of methods through which the training agenda will be delivered; however, while this may be at the organization's site there may be valid reasons for another venue, for example if benchmarking against another external organization or joint collaboration – in such circumstances a neutral territory may prove more appropriate. Indeed, the provision of a conducive training environment and facilities, along with the alignment of the learning activities with the business needs, should deliver improved performance in customer standards, commercial awareness and technical operations and in supporting the organization's identified change programme to meet its identified business needs.

Organizational implementation: During Phase 1, the first of the organizational changes will have been prepared which can then be implemented as part of this second phase. The identification of positions within the organizational structure and the match to existing employees will be undertaken as part of the task analysis and job profiling exercise in this phase. As the organization's task analysis is completed, further appointments can be made and the organizational structure may also change again during the final third phase.

HR environment: To achieve its mission, vision and objectives, any organization must seek to realize the full potential of all of its employees to ensure that it is seen to be a "preferred" employer within the community and is able to contribute to business performance financial growth. By valuing its staff, the organization in this second phase will enhance its creativity and its ability to adapt to change, and increase its overall performance. Achieving these business objectives will contribute to improving its competitive position and increase the prospects of growing the business further.

Organizational health and safety: The primary and continuing policy of any company is that, in the conduct of its business, it will need to continue to achieve standards of health and safety for its employees, customers and others affected by its business operations that are equivalent to best practice in each area of its activities. To achieve the requirements of this business policy, the company may initiate a number of objectives to be fulfilled, both in terms of legal requirements and to satisfy the organization's own standards. These objectives are likely to be:

- to ensure that all employees are aware of their responsibilities for health and safety standards
- to encourage the active participation of all members of staff in continuously improving their work environment;
- to ensure that all contractors, suppliers and others undertaking activities for the business are briefed on their health and safety obligations and responsibilities and also that they thereafter operate proper systems to ensure that standards are maintained;
- to analyse continuously the risks faced by the organization and prepare, update and revise systems of work and emergency plans to meet such risks.

Phase 3: Ongoing support and consolidation phase:
The final phase will typically last for a further 18

months following on from Phase 2 and will need to concentrate on continual support and improvements as the changes become embedded within the organization and are regarded as the organization's new culture. This longer-term third phase is important for the changes to be successfully accepted within the transformed organizational structure and for employees to understand their roles and contribute to future performance of the business. The main activities in this final phase are as follows.

Communication: Continued employee involvement and consultation through a rolling communications programme will need to be developed in this final phase to assure the employees of the importance of the changes, how they can be involved and how they can support the changes to the business. In addition, the organization's management will need to assist this process further through open dialogues with staff and by conducting research into their concerns and reacting to the findings.

Training review and feedback: In order to ensure that the training provided is up to date and relevant, a review of all provisions should be conducted at the end of each business plan year. All employees who have attended any type of training should be encouraged to give feedback on its success – this should be seen to be of value to management and not just the completion of the "happy sheets" so often witnessed in large organizations. As the changes mature, consideration may also be given to the implementation of a total quality management (TQM) approach as part of a drive for improved performance through technology and increased staff competency and performance standards.

HR environment: In the third phase, the HR director will typically need to work with all parties to develop a series of HR policies that reflect both the current conditions and the future goals of the company. These will cover, for example, staff forums and grievance procedures, reward policy, succession planning, health and safety, corporate responsibility and ethics. While striving to achieve the goals of the organization, the HR function will need to remain alert and prepared to respond from an organizational perspective to any potential external threats and opportunities which may support or hinder the organization's business performance.

Succession planning: The earlier job analysis from Phase 2 can be used to identify key post-holder replacements and job profiles containing the principal activities and accountabilities together with their associated competencies and technical knowledge. This can be used as the foundation of selection for new jobs and vacancies after the change transition. A lack of a strategic approach to succession planning will expose key organizational roles and skills to significant risk within the context of the future operating structure. At this final stage, the senior management team will need to understand "change" in totality and must be equipped to manage the unforeseen impacts of natural attrition and loss of key members of the organizational team for career development reasons. Active succession planning is one of the approaches aimed at alleviating these operational and business risks.

MANAGING CHANGE AND PEOPLE

Having looked at some approaches to change, its impact on the many aspects of the organization, planning change and now the components of a large-scale change programme, this chapter now moves to present three models around managing the resistance to change. With few exceptions, people's reaction to change will follow the change curve shown in Figure 2.8, itself influenced by issues around security, status and self esteem.

Clearly, implementing change needs to be planned, executed, reported and reviewed for it to be successful and appropriate to the business. The change curve is sometimes referred to as the "loss transition curve" and was derived by Dr Elizabeth Kübler-Ross's studies into bereavement, first published in 1969 and later embraced as part of organizational management theory. Before considering change – what type of change, how to do it, identifying

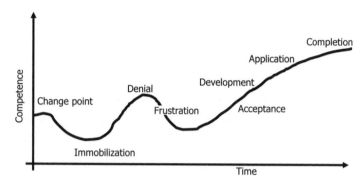

Figure 2.8 Change curve.
(From *The Essential Management Toolbox: Tools, Models and Notes for Managers and Consultants.* S.A. Burtonshaw-Gunn, 2008, reproduced with permission.)

who is to be involved or who is affected by any changes – two points need to be made. First, it is absolutely crucial to gain the most senior level support, ownership and commitment as any change management plan is destined to fail unless visibly supported by the senior management of the organization. Second, acceptance is needed within the organization that such recommended change is seen as being appropriate for the specific organization. On this basis, acceptance by the management of integrated business plan objectives will then allow them to consider the type of change strategy best suited to pursue a new direction or initiate changes necessary to facilitate increased organizational performance.

In agreeing an appropriate strategy, or combination of strategies, for change, the organization's management will need to take into account the following factors:

- The urgency of the situation.
- The degree of the opposition expected.
- The power base of the change initiator.
- The existing transparency of information and ease of communication.
- Demonstrable examples of commitment to integrated planning during the change programme.
- The nature of the current organization's culture and its likely response to change.

While there are a number of models to assist individuals in the change process, it should be noted that reactions to change can be categorized as one of four groups. These categories range from those individuals who openly resist the change and may even try to prevent it to those who merely go along with the change but may not be committed to being part of its success. The four categories of resistance are described below:

- **Protesters:** Who openly make their objections known to the organization and colleagues; however, once issues are identified they can be considered and managed.
- **Zombies:** Have no strong opinion and are happy to go along with any proposed changes without offering any constructive comment.
- **Saboteurs:** Like to show that the old ways were fine, openly find fault with any new systems or process change and seek opportunities to make the change fail.

- **Survivors:** Accept the change and make best use of any new situation for their own advantage.

Knowledge of these groups can help managers to recognize an individual's resistance to change and hence provide a better chance of managing the change process without further resistance. Indeed, the level of resistance to change is normally related to the magnitude of the change required and while there are often issues around perceived job security the level of resistance influences the speed of the undertaking. Figure 2.9 presents a matrix of emotional issues which provides some guidance in addressing resistance and adoptability to the planned changes.

Figure 2.10 is the third model with respect to resistance to change and covers the relationship between change and security which re-emphasizes some common

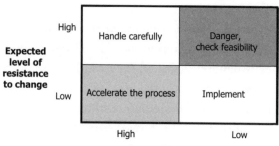

Figure 2.9   Matrix of emotional issues.
(From *The Ten Keys to Successful Change Management*. J. Pendlebury *et al.*, 1998, reproduced with permission.)

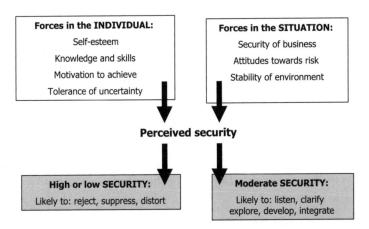

Figure 2.10 Security and change.
(From *The Essential Management Toolbox: Tools, Models and Notes for Managers and Consultants.* S.A. Burtonshaw-Gunn, 2008, reproduced with permission.)

factors that play a role in perceived security together with typical respondents' behaviour. For those involved in initiating or implementing a change programme, knowledge of the perceived security issues needs to be understood as this will aid communications and allow the most appropriate approach to be selected aimed at gaining support from those affected.

Forces – both within individuals and within organizations – contribute to the degree of security and can promote feelings of either insecurity or high security. In turn, these feelings can lead to contrasting responses to the planned organizational change. As such, it is important to recognize that the forces that contribute to the culture and the attitudes of the individuals within the organization are key to establishing a high degree of security which will support a positive response to organizational change and hence contribute to future business performance. The factors contributing to culture and individual performance are discussed later in Figure 4.3.

From the models described in this chapter, it would not be an exaggeration to say that there is no other topic in management that impacts on the whole of the business operation as much as change management and consequential organizational development: from business planning, production, improvement processes, quality systems; from marketing through to customer relationship management; and from a personnel viewpoint covering both individual performance and team working. The topic of change and organizational development (OD) should not be merely considered to be the production of a company's organogram – it is clearly far more that this. Organizational development involves understanding the culture of the company, identifying it strengths and opportunities and trying to minimize its weakness and any real (or perceived) threats throughout the whole company.

Having discussed some models around change and OD it has to be said that "change" *per se* has now become a regular feature of business life as part of the desire for continual increased business performance and the ever-important need to demonstrate a growth in shareholder value. However, change management strategies have quite often been too rapidly internalized and wrongly communicated, usually resulting in a knee-jerk response which links demand for increased performance purely with the consequential financial benefits. It is stressed that successful management of the resistance to change reflected in the earlier quotation from *The Prince* by Machiavelli published almost 500 years ago is the critical factor to achieving any degree of long-term and lasting success. While it may be difficult to undertake change, the words of President John F. Kennedy suggest that those that fail to embrace change will have a limited future with his statement: "Change is the law of life and those who look only to the past or present are certain to miss the future". Perhaps this is also a good message for today's business managers.

For change to succeed, a corporately social environment needs to be fostered which truly encourages and rewards organizational leaders for maintaining high organizational performance and promoting the right behavioural environment, culture and values. Implementation of change often results in periods of organizational tension, however; in that state of flux those leading the change management process must not mistakenly overlook the huge return on investment to business from harnessing the intuitive skills of its most valuable resource – its people. Change can only become successful when people are engaged and committed to its planned outcomes (see also Chapter 3).

It is also worth noting that without careful consideration of the interconnectedness of the behavioural factors that affect so much of an organization's culture, any lasting improved performance will become an elusive goal and any related change in culture will have no lasting value and thus be transient in its nature. Therefore, improved organizational performance is about not only the application of hard and fast rules for achievement, but rather an acceptance and ownership of the impact these factors have in shaping organizational behaviours during periods of change. If change management objectives and performance management targets are not seen to be remotely achievable they can unintentionally prevent organizations creating the conditions necessary for gaining an improved and sustainable performance while fuelling at the same time Machiavellian protectionist and defensive behaviours.

CHAPTER 3

PEOPLE-FOCUSED PERFORMANCE MANAGEMENT

DRIVERS FOR PERFORMANCE MANAGEMENT

Before looking at the role of "people and performance" it is useful to remember that within both commerce and industry the *raison d'être* for the senior level of management, normally the board of directors, is to examine the nature of the business and steer the company on its future course. Such direction requires the establishment and implementation of a robust strategy, which will be primarily concerned with the company as a whole. Indeed, such corporate strategy formulation will inevitably have to consider its present business role, the future business direction it should take and how the board's vision and objectives can be successfully implemented and achieved. This task of strategy development involves decisions on plans at the most senior level which recognize both the financial and organizational development of the company with such major decision-making regarded as being at the very heart of strategic management. Development of a corporate strategy should not be regarded as an isolated

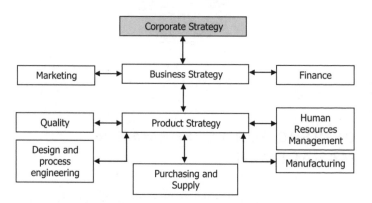

Figure 3.1 Relationship between external facing business strategies and internally focused product strategy.
(From *The Essential Management Toolbox: Tools, Models and Notes for Managers and Consultants*. S.A. Burtonshaw-Gunn, 2008, reproduced with permission.)

senior task as it must be inter-related with other strategies, as shown in Figure 3.1.

To achieve any degree of success many writers on the topic of strategic management stress that the organization's corporate vision must be aligned to its core values; to the organization's mission; and to its goals and the objectives it wishes to pursue in the short, medium and long term. In general, it is also recognized that of absolute prime importance to any company – irrespective of its size, or its public/private ownership state – must be its desire to survive over the long term. This may be achieved by balancing the need to earn an economic profit (and satisfy its shareholders) with the need to invest in its own resources: whether they are systems, processes, plant, machinery or its employees. The efficient use of these "human resources" largely governs the success of the organization as it is ultimately reliant on its employees to both formulate and implement strategy. Strategic management may therefore involve the development, review and remoulding of the organizational structure that will best ensure survival within its operating environment, as shown in the strategic relationship model of Figure 3.1. In addition, organizations wishing to take a long-term view will need to consider the training, education and development of their employees, especially their managers, as a core element of successful alignment.

In looking at the development of organizational performance measures, many leading companies have for a period embraced the European Foundation of Quality

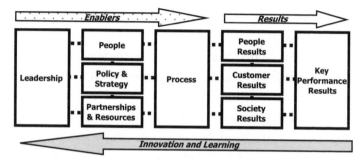

Figure 3.2 The EFQM Business Excellence Model.
(© European Foundation of Quality Management, reproduced with permission.)

Management (EFQM) Business Excellence Model (Figure 3.2) which identifies four categories of business results – Key Performance Results (Financial), Society, People and, within the mechanics of the model, the most important category of Customer Results. These quantitative results are underpinned and driven by a series of five qualitative "enablers" comprising Leadership, People, Policy, Partnership and Process Management.

While there is naturally a range of initiatives to improve on all of these categories, the topic of performance management has traditionally focused on the HR aspects, as planned improvement in the People category can provide a subsequent impact across many of the other categories of the EFQM model.

Complementary to the Business Excellence Model there has been an increasing interest in performance indicators and performance-based balanced scorecard tools which measure the performance of the company through assessment and monitoring aimed at assisting in decision-making and contributing to the organization's long-term success. Establishing performance indicators typically covers financial and non-financial measurements and impacts on operational management (corporate objective setting, performance assessment, etc.) and those in HR management (*inter alia* training and career development, succession planning, reward systems, competency management, etc.). It has to be said that the increasing growth in industry benchmarking is made easier when companies use the same measurements on which to assess their performance and compare their results against other well-regarded companies. The use of performance indicators (PIs) for this purpose has seen wide acceptance and support in the UK construction industry, for example, which publishes industry performance data, and has over the last decade established regional best practice clubs and knowledge-sharing initiatives.

PERFORMANCE AND COMPETENCY DEVELOPMENT

The focus of this chapter now moves to discuss the importance of the required behavioural factors as a key enabler in developing and embedding a high performance culture within an organization. Although it is very difficult to encapsulate fully the vast nature of this topic, the need to understand the "people dimension" is a vital part of the corporate management of the organization. Whatever the industry and size of business, profit levels, or markets in which it operates, almost without exception the annual report of every organization will make reference to its employees as being the business's most valuable asset. However, in many cases not only are these also its most expensive asset but are absolutely central to the rate at which organizational performance can be increased.

On the premise that the often quoted "People are our greatest assets" statement is true then to support enhanced job performance this "great" asset needs to be effective in four areas:

- **Competencies:** How they go about their work.
- **Attitude:** How they prepare for work.
- **Skills:** What they can do.
- **Knowledge:** What they know.

It is the proficiency in these four areas which contributes to the business's performance and which can be applied to a number of activities within an organization such as those associated with customer focus, communications, team-working, innovation and problem solving to name but a few. The development of competencies, attitudes, skills and knowledge is linked into the individual's performance as shown in Figure 3.3, which suggests a closer working relationship between HR and functional managers as part of a cyclical business process. Investment in the training and development aspects of the model may

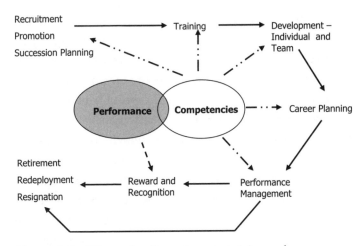

Figure 3.3   The cycle of recruitment, training and career management as part of a performance management system.
(From *The Essential Management Toolbox: Tools, Models and Notes for Managers and Consultants*. S.A. Burtonshaw-Gunn, 2008, reproduced with permission.)

be undertaken as part of a wider programme of competency management with objectives around the above four areas.

For many companies using a competency management system there is a clear linkage to their training provision and a typical five-phase systematic approach to training (SAT) used by a number of the more regulated industries such as oil and gas, nuclear, rail and others. This five-phase process is described below.

Phase 1 involves an *analysis* to develop a detailed understanding of the task that an individual is required to undertake and requires an assessor to capture information on how the task is performed and the competencies that are needed to perform the task. This information is usually gathered from procedures, expert knowledge and, where applicable to the industry setting, any regulatory requirements.

Phase 2 covers the *design phase*, which focuses on the development of a suite of training aims and objectives that are directly based on the competencies identified during Phase 1. This helps to ensure that the training is subsequently developed to directly support the trainee in achieving the required competencies for their job/role. It should be recognized that staff will have varied backgrounds and as such may attain required competencies via alternative routes. The aim of the training is to reconcile the competencies identified for the task with the competencies of the trainee. It is recommended that each training objective clearly specifies:

- who the objective is aimed at;
- what skill is being trained;
- on what piece of equipment;
- under which conditions; and
- to which performance standard.

All of these can be written up as training plans.

Phase 3 takes the *training plan* and develops this into the necessary training material required to deliver the training. Typically, the material required will include training aids, handouts, assessment methodologies and their associated competence assessment criteria.

Phase 4 covers the *delivery* of the training to meet the identified requirement. If effort is put into the previous development phases then the training should be delivered consistently and reliably to all attendees.

Phase 5 covers the *review* of the process and the management of training records. In order to control expenditure and resources all training programmes should have local management approval prior to the start of the training programme as local management is often responsible for controlling a regular evaluation review of training; typically on an annual basis. In some industries, long-term retention requirements apply to covering the training records, which will necessitate their storage and archiving.

It should be the responsibility of local supervision, e.g. team leader, local manager or project manager, to identify the assessment and the roles, tasks and training needs in conjunction with the individual as part of any performance management system (see also Figure 3.6). For those involved in supporting the performance objectives and staff development through the provision of necessary and identified training, the following information should be gathered as part of the training management process:

- Identification of the role of an individual or group of co-workers.

- Identification of the tasks where skilled, qualified and experienced staff are needed.
- For each task, identification of the specific performance competencies required, including experience requirements in line with required performance standards.
- Identification of which individuals are required to undertake key tasks.
- Identification of any training needs by comparing the existing identified competencies and experience of the trainees with the competencies and experience identified above.

Undertaking the collection of the above information can be used to produce a simple matrix of individuals assessed against the required competencies and the training identified. In addition, listing competencies explicitly can enable the skills and knowledge needed to perform certain roles and tasks to be fully identified. These competencies can then be assessed to demonstrate the level of a person's competence for each area that they are required to perform. In many cases, this approach will follow a three-step process covering: the identification of the competencies needed for a role or task; a performance standard for each competency; and the assessment of the role-holder.

The table shown as Figure 3.4 provides some useful guidance in selecting the most appropriate assessment method for those undertaking job and task assessments.

Method	Strengths	Weaknesses	Key issues
Observing someone carrying out their job by on-the-job training and assessment.	▪ Provides high quality evidence. ▪ Assessment can be undertaken as part of line manager's job. ▪ Individuals become familiar with ongoing assessment. ▪ Provides continuous assessment basis. ▪ Evidence is produced regardless of whether it is used for assessment.	▪ Opportunities to demonstrate competence across full range of activities may be limited. ▪ Assessors may be too overloaded to carry out assessments. ▪ Assessor/trainee relationship. ▪ Needs to be managed to reduce any disruption to the workforce.	▪ Need for trained assessors. ▪ Advantages in using multiple assessors. ▪ Need for clear lines of communication and QA measures. ▪ Need to have a checklist of what to observe.
Specially set tasks: skills, tests, simulations, projects, assignments.	▪ When normal work activity observation is not possible, special tasks or assignments can be set to generate the required evidence. ▪ A useful tool for generating evidence. ▪ Can be off-site and therefore avoid noisy or disruptive environments. ▪ Test conditions can be standardized for skill tests. ▪ Time for testing can be effectively allocated.	▪ Removed from realistic working conditions. ▪ Individuals may act differently in test situations. ▪ Structure of projects or assignments is loose. ▪ Difficult to predict the exact type of evidence that will be generated. ▪ Need to recognize that this evidence may not be of high quality. ▪ Can be expensive and time consuming.	▪ Need for good planning and clear structure. ▪ Need to ensure a valid and appropriate simulation.
Oral questioning to supplement evidence of performance by asking questions to find out about performance in a different context or in other circumstances.	▪ Valuable tool for collecting evidence across full range of activities. ▪ Useful to investigate underpinning knowledge. ▪ Can be rigorous and standardized.	▪ Assessors often answer their own questions. ▪ Not sufficient in itself to demonstrate competence. ▪ Least likely to reflect or represent real working conditions.	▪ Need assessors trained in questioning techniques. ▪ Requires inferential jump.
Written examination.	▪ Valuable for knowledge-based activities.	▪ Also assesses ability to write and construct written.	▪ Danger that "knowing" is confused with being.

Figure 3.4 Assessment methods. Encouraging performance from people development.

Method	Strengths	Weaknesses	Key issues
	• Can be well structured to elicit key areas of knowledge and understanding.	material. • Needs skilled assessors to judge. • Lacks validity. • Time burden for all involved.	able to do it. • Often unstructured or unplanned. • Supplies supplementary evidence of actual performance
Multiple choice papers.	• Well-designed questions can be standardized. • Elicits key knowledge/ understanding in short timescale. • Easy to mark/ assess.	• Always a probability of the correct answer being chosen randomly. • Needs careful design. • Time away from work required. • Difficult to provide feedback if test is reused with same trainee.	• Time and skills needed for design, delivery and marking. • Supplementary evidence only – not direct evidence of actual performance.
Aptitude tests. Typically include verbal reasoning, numerical reasoning, logic, etc.	• Quick and easy to apply. • Well-designed questions can be standardized. • Useful to determine whether people have the underlying competency to carry out a job.	• Always a certain probability of the correct answer being chosen at random. • Needs careful design.	• Does not provide evidence of actual job performance. • Mixed levels of predictive ability.
Psychometric tests. Tests designed to consider the psychological characteristics of individuals and match these to a particular post.	• Quick and easy to apply. • Particularly useful for certain tasks where they are well established and the required characteristics are well established.	• Needs certain levels of expertise to ensure appropriate tests are selected for the post. • Needs careful design. • Danger that people labelled. • Measures characteristics that influence behaviour but not how a person behaves when using these characteristics.	• Does not provide evidence of actual job performance – not direct measure of competence. • Mixed levels of predictive ability.
Assessment Development Centres.	• High quality end result. • Provides an opportunity for many of the methods to be used such as role play, exercises, assessed interviews, etc.	• Can be costly and have high time demands for trainees and assessors.	• The efficacy depends on the quality of the assessment methods used.

Figure 3.4 *Continued*

Performance management would not be complete without mentioning the topic of pay as a component of the "reward and recognition" element shown in Figure 3.3. Many organizations believe that when performance management is linked to an individual's remuneration then the quality of the performance discussions at the review time often deteriorates. Even for those trying to separate these two topics, performance management is often linked with performance-related pay (PRP) at the more senior staff levels of an organization. It has to be said that PRP is widely regarded as an important element in many performance management schemes because it strengthens the message that performance and competence are important and offers a mechanism to reward people according to their performance, contribution or competence. On the other hand, there is also a corresponding view that performance-related pay can inhibit teamwork because of its individualistic nature, and as such can lead to the demotivation of some team members through their perceptions of the performance and disparate reward of other team members.

It should now be clear that for performance management to provide tangible benefits there must be a common acceptance across an organization that this topic is a serious business feature, not just as a process but also in conjunction with recognition and respect for people as a key contributor to an organization's performance. As such, processes and people both need to have a mutual respect for one another if performance management is to have

Figure 3.5 Mutual objective setting and performance management.
(From *Management Concepts and Practices*. Dr Tim Hannagan, 2005, reproduced with permission of Pearson Education.)

any chance of succeeding as a business driver. Putting training matched to individual objective setting into practice and linking this to performance management is the model shown in Figure 3.5.

To some extent this cyclic model follows the traditional quality management "plan–do–check–act" approach, showing progression from agreeing the objectives to discussing performance with joint actions which managers and staff need to instigate with a view to improving individual and hence organizational performance. In setting action plans and development opportunities for individuals, it will also be important to have some understanding of learning styles as identified by Honey and

Mumford in the 1980s and how the individuals' preferences can be best utilized. A number of tools that may be used in performance management are discussed below. The process of objective setting is often used either on an annual basis or on a task basis as appropriate. Setting realistic and achievable objectives can be used to improve performance although for maximum benefit the plan–do–check–act process should also be used to support periodic review and monitoring.

- **Performance measurement approaches:** Individual and team performance should be capable of being linked to an understandable reporting model. One of these is the use of a "balanced scorecard", which comprises a set of measures that examines the business from customer, internal, learning and financial perspectives. Another is the EFQM Excellence Model, as shown earlier in Figure 3.2, which indicates that employee satisfaction, customer satisfaction and the company's impact on society are achieved through leadership and other financial performance indicators.
- **Performance and development reviews:** While PDRs may be used in the management of an organization's performance, even those companies without performance management systems tend to operate staff appraisals in which managers regularly review staff performance, their potential and identify their development needs. Those organizations with PDRs

also use this time to reflect on the individual's past performance as a basis for making development and improvement plans. Review meetings must be constructive and be conducted in an open, free-flowing and honest way and where the reviewee is encouraged to do most of the talking. At the same time as reviewing competent technical performance, a number of organizations may also choose to conduct an assessment of the individual's behavioural competencies as part of their performance management system. Such a behavioural assessment can provide another tool for measuring individual performance and for providing development activities to help employees further reinforce their technical skills and interpersonal competencies to reflect the organization's required practice standards.

- **360-degree feedback:** This review mechanism consists of performance data generated from a number of sources and usually includes feedback from those staff to whom the individual reports, his/her peer group, their staff and – very importantly – their customers. It also typically includes a self-assessment using the same process as others are commenting on to allow the individual's own perceptions of their performance to be compared with these other assessing groups. The 360-degree feedback approach is commonly used as part of a self-development or management development programme where a more rounded view of the individual is required and with less bias than if such an assessment is conducted only by the individual's immediate manager.

- **Teamworking:** For many organizations teamworking has become an important part of contributing to their business success. In instances where projects justifiably allow for team membership to be long term then team performance (output, customer service and satisfaction, and financial results) can be measured. However, these will require team members to agree on their objectives and receive feedback on their individual contribution to the team and/or project.

- **Objectives and performance standards:** In a typical performance management process both the manager and the individual need to agree on a number of objectives or goals that can be undertaken by the individual, department and organization over a period of time, usually in a one-year period in line with the appraisal or performance review timescales. These objectives can be both work related, referring to the results to be attained, or personal objectives, taking the form of developmental objectives for individuals. In both cases, however, objectives must be regarded as "SMART" (Specific, Measurable, Agreed, Realistic and Time Bound) and may be expressed as targets to be met or tasks to be completed. In more recent times, some companies have added an additional "T" to make "SMARTT" where this addition refers to the term "Traceable" which also reflects common quality assurance practices. In addition to these objectives are performance standards which may be used when it is not possible to set time-based targets, or if there is a continuing objective of the job which does not change significantly from one review period to the next. Setting SMART objectives, reviewing performance and providing feedback to individuals are stages of the typical performance management process shown in Figure 3.6.

1. Objective setting
- Individual clear when to perform and what is expected
- Performance targets, measures and standards exist
- Seen as attainable by individual

6. Recognition
- Positive if performance is as expected
- If performance is not up to standard identify problem and communicate need for improvement

2. The individual
- Capability to perform as desired – skills and knowledge
- Willing to perform

5. Performance monitoring
- Interim reviews of performance
- Identify interim targets
- Take action to remedy poor performance as necessary

3. Resources
- People
- Equipment, materials
- Information
- Plans
- Money

4. Feedback
- Relevant, immediate and frequent
- Constructive, balanced and specific
- Focused on critical success factors of task behaviour

Figure 3.6 Typical cycle of a performance management process. (From *The Essential Management Toolbox: Tools, Models and Notes for Managers and Consultants*. S.A. Burtonshaw-Gunn, 2008, reproduced with permission.)

- **Coaching:** For some staff, coaching is an important tool in learning and developing an individual's skills and knowledge. It can result in improved job performance and the achievement of wider organizational objectives for the individual and is increasingly being regarded as the responsibility of an individual's immediate manager. Coaching can often link in well as part of the individual's learning and development and as part of their performance and development review. Unlike the performance review process coaching usually takes place throughout the year and often features as one of a range of approaches covering executive development ranging from the directive, company mandated requirements on executives through to a number of more empathetic approaches such as coaching, supporting and counselling on an "as and when required" basis. The range of approaches is shown in Figure 3.7.

- **Learning and development:** In almost every business the main route to improved organizational performance is the development of the skills and

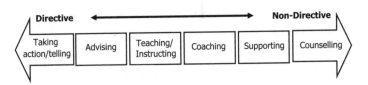

Figure 3.7 Continuum of executive development approaches. (From *The Role of Strategic Executive Development*. S.A. Burtonshaw-Gunn and M.G. Salameh, ICAFI University Press, 2007b.)

competencies of its staff. This requires an understanding of the processes and techniques of organizational, team and individual learning and the performance and development review is often the best time when individuals can be encouraged to think about which ways they wish to develop. This can lead to establishing a personal development plan with agreed actions, budgets and support requirements on which staff can develop themselves in line with the company's business objectives. Away from company initiated development, people-focused performance management can also include self-managed learning (SML) which is widely regarded as a process whereby individuals determine what they learn and how they may learn with others in the context of their own (unique) situation.

In looking at the final above point, it is important to consider the context within which learning and development resides within an organization. This is true if there exists a continuum of aspirations ranging from economic survival, through to maintenance and business growth, with success at any of these stages predicated on the right organizational development decisions being made. Of course, while this argument can be applied to all levels of an organization, it is often the senior management who need to have the necessary abilities to contribute to setting and being accountable for achievement of the organization's corporate goals and performance. To appreciate how these decisions can be effectively focused, it is important to understand how learning and development needs can be prioritized. Typically, these development needs fall into the three groupings of maintenance, strategic and career needs which are described below and are aligned to the "MoSCow: must-do, should-do, could-do" approach:

- **Maintenance needs:** These are the needs that the organization must address in order to stay in business, for example: employment legislation, heath and safety regulations, corporate taxation liabilities, etc. Generally, maintenance needs are considered as the "must-do's" of any business and usually comprise a top-up of knowledge and skills to support a steady state operational environment.

- **Strategic needs:** These cover the type of needs that should be addressed in order to achieve the corporate goals, some of which will more than likely be centred on business improvement or change management. Examples of strategic needs may include increasing service provision standards and the introduction of new technology, products or services. In contrast to the maintenance needs, strategic needs can be regarded as organizational "should-do's", generally because they tend to relate to business transformation activities relying on the development of new knowledge, skills and even attitudes in order to manage business transition and transformation activities effectively.

- **Career needs:** These needs relate to an organizational mindset regarding investing and developing people so that over time they can make a more effective contribution to current and future strategic plans. In this category examples include the need to continuously develop and maintain a level of domain-specific experienced managers with the right competency profiles. In prioritizing learning and development, it is often the career needs which are typically thought of as optional and consequently the "could-do's". These tend to realize a payback to an organization over the mid to longer term and, in many instances, may be driven as much by the individual's aspirations as any direct organizational requirements. However, this is not to suggest that career needs are unimportant; on the contrary they are often a critical element in supporting the organization's ability to stay competitive and achieve growth.

Having established these three groupings, and understood them from a demand and planning perspective, it is then essential to establish where the right balance lies for a particular organization. It is interesting to note that "learning organizations" try to anticipate some of these needs from the strategic goals and targets – and by examining, capturing and prioritizing individual aspirations. This is crucial if the talent within the business is to be retained and developed, and as such will require the strategic leaders to consider the organization's development needs in integrated terms rather than in a timeframe merely matched to any short-term performance objectives. Focusing on the businesses strategic needs as the main process should be seen as the key driver although in times when the business plan concentrates on consolidation, rather than growth, an opportunity for an organization to support more SML may be appropriate. While consideration may be given to the three categories of learning needs, it should be noted that there are also other factors which often come into play in assessing the strategic role of learning and development as shown in Figure 3.8.

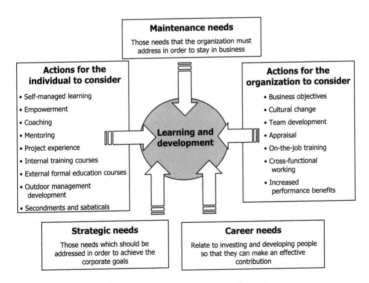

Figure 3.8 Learning and development considerations. (From *The Role of Strategic Executive Development*. S.A. Burtonshaw-Gunn and M.G. Salameh, ICAFI University Press, 2007b.)

PERFORMANCE THROUGH EMPOWERMENT

The final area of people performance of this chapter is that from the empowerment of teams or individuals by managers. While individual teams may have a degree of empowerment from their immediate manager, it is clear that for full empowerment covering rewards, goal setting, appraisals, etc., empowerment has to be driven from the top of the organization to become part of the company's culture and business philosophy. The table showing the features of traditional and empowered organizations (Figure 3.9) examines the incentives and controls in an empowered company contrasting with those of a traditional organization.

While many companies may wish to empower their employees this presents problems not for those empowered but more often for their managers who consider this as a "loss of control" while recognizing the benefits of empowerment. Against such a dichotomy, the 19th century US fairground phrase "close but no cigar" can be aptly applied, meaning that while the intentions were valid and appropriate, their implementation is less mature. Examples of the "no cigar" expression abound within organizations and can be witnessed in almost every aspect of business management which, unfortunately, often serve to hinder the acceptance of the performance management philosophy and the investment made in its intro-

	Traditional	Empowered
Executives	• Make decisions • Review results • Control firm's responses	• Delegate decisions • Plan for the future • Develop vision
Managers	• Supervise people • Monitor activity • Make work assignments • Report to the top	• Support team building • Manage systems • Coach teams • Report to the top
Rewards are	• Primary extrinsic (money and benefits) • Little intrinsic possible	• Lean to intrinsic (but extrinsic often equal to traditional) • Business results
Basis for pay	• Job duties performed • People supervised	• Team output • Variable salary
People receive	• Fixed salary • Small bonuses (pay for behaviour)	• Large bonuses (pay to performance) • Critical activity
Vision setting	• Limited activity	• Bottom-up process
Goal setting	• Top-down activity	• Customers have input
Performance appraisal	• Supervisor/manager only • Closely guarded process • One to one assessment	• Team mates may share • May have team assessment • Uses result-based performance data
Choosing leaders	• Relies on managerial judgement • Boss/bosses appointed to lead work groups • Critical management activity	• Leadership rotates inside a work team • Personal control is much less important

Figure 3.9 Features of traditional and empowered organizations. (From *The Essential Management Toolbox: Tools, Models and Notes for Managers and Consultants. S.A. Burtonshaw-Gunn, 2008, reproduced with permission.*)

duction and ongoing administration. To counter this, it is stressed that there must be common acceptance across organizations – irrespective of their size, market position or ownership status – that the topic of performance management requires professionally trained managers with an ability to think in business performance terms, to make strategic decisions and look to the wider implications of management decisions than just as a mere custodian of the company's processes. Indeed, key to the successful introduction and ongoing application of performance management is having:

- a clear understanding about the process and what it is meant to contribute to the business.
- an understanding of the current organization and how it should function in a high-performance culture.
- a recognition that individuals will need to be focused and assigned mutually agreed SMART objectives for them to "buy in" to performance management and play their part.
- an understanding that, although a performance management system may be documented and capable of being deployed widely across an organization, the other aspects of business cannot be ignored or treated in isolation if the "close but no cigar" criticism is to be avoided.

While performance management is about developing and implementing appropriate business processes, it also needs the support of people – as previously mentioned and widely heralded as a company's key asset. It is suggested that for an organization to gain the maximum value from a performance management system it has to be configured to functionally operate in a predictive way. This provides a capability for strategic leaders to analyse the performance hierarchy to pinpoint the source of any underperformance within their organization and implement appropriate corrective actions through support, development and training. However, it must be stressed that for any performance-based measurement system to really add value and contribute to an organization's performance there should be a reliance on operating a no-blame culture where it is safe to highlight sources of poor performance variance not as a criticism but as a proactive opportunity to improve.

For those tasked with introducing or using a performance management system, the focus should be on achieving the right balance between managing processes and managing people to achieve the right behavioural environment and maintaining sustainability. This balance is not easy to achieve in practice and will necessitate the continuous engagement of every employee to play their part in the performance management process and nurture their emotional investment in the business. Simply relying on quantitative methods will not provide the answers for achieving and maintaining a high performance culture, but in conjunction with a qualitative appreciation of the behavioural elements discussed above there will be an increase in the probability of successfully managing people's expectations through their perceived psychological contracts. On a final point, it should be noted that, like cultural change management discussed in Chapter 2, performance management requires time and investment to implement and provide the benefits in line with its full potential. However, if this is done in a half-hearted way without considering and addressing the other complementary issues of the business, then a lack of commitment will manifest itself in poor performance results, increased staff turnover and low levels of motivation. Addressing the important "close but no cigar" issues with the requisite balance of both process and people management must be considered to be a vital element to maintain and increase people-focused performance management.

CHAPTER 4

KNOWLEDGE MANAGEMENT AND PERFORMANCE

DEVELOPMENTS IN KNOWLEDGE MANAGEMENT

Although the term "knowledge management" is now in widespread use, it originated from the development of systems for managing knowledge which gained prominence in the 1980s. At this time there was a focus on artificial intelligence (AI) and expert systems; in turn, these provided concepts such as "knowledge acquisition", "knowledge engineering" and "knowledge-base systems". The term "knowledge management" itself was introduced in the popular press in the early 1990s followed later by arguably the most widely read work on the topic to date, Nonaka and Takeuchi's book *The Knowledge-Creating Company: How Japanese Companies Create the Dynamics of Innovation.* This interest was witnessed by a growing number of knowledge management conferences and seminars as organizations explored managing and leveraging explicit, potential and tacit knowledge in an attempt to achieve a competitive advantage. Typically, these three principal types of knowledge exist within most businesses and can be generally defined as:

- **Explicit or transferable knowledge:** This relates to information recorded within hard copy documents or management information systems (MIS).
- **Tacit knowledge:** This refers to the information that employees and stakeholders retain in their heads and as such is not documented.
- **Potential knowledge:** This is generally the repository of raw data that an organization holds within its information systems, which often lies dormant.

For most organizations wishing to improve or achieve higher performance, the objective has traditionally been to utilize their physical assets by envisioning innovative ways of operating them at an optimal level. Generally speaking, the same principles hold true for knowledge management – with the key difference being that knowledge is an intangible asset and as such requires other considerations to stimulate ways of working it harder to deliver increased value to a business. Quite often tangible assets such as buildings, plant and machinery appear easier to manage because they actually exist in a physical form; consequently, any impact on their performance can be addressed through established business management tools such as benchmarking, sharing best practice and implementation of cultural change management programmes, or alternatively deployment of business continuity plans to cover a myriad of potential scenarios. Research has shown, however, that these physical assets often have less capacity to create and deliver new value to a business than that of the knowledge residing within the business itself.

Historically, information – whether in the form of raw data or in an analysed form – has always needed to be managed in order to increase its use or capitalize on any potential time-related value. It is not surprising then to learn that knowledge management has its routes in data and document management which established the primary necessity to ensure that decision-making information and ideas were filtered, prioritized and presented in the most accessible and timely manner. However, with the advent of shared data environments and open networks, innovative new ideas and capitalizing on problem solving in the public domain has made a number of pioneering organizations realize the huge scale of the potential and untapped knowledge reserves they may have hidden and with it performance benefits from sharing knowledge.

ORGANIZATIONS AND KNOWLEDGE MANAGEMENT

It has to be said that over the years many companies have been trying to develop techniques to capture and share knowledge across their operations. In this regard, organizations often view knowledge management as a relationship between people, technology, processes, strategy and a cultural context and on this basis usually consider that it requires inputs from HRM, strategic management, organizational studies and IT systems. The initial challenge for many organizations eager to adopt knowledge management to stimulate innovation and growth has been in bringing these together to establish initially what they already know. Typically, the most easily accessible knowledge within any business is the "potential knowledge" in the form of raw data. However, the level of difficulty increases markedly for any business when attempting the acquisition of "tacit knowledge" and its accompanying synthesis by the organization's leadership population. This higher level of analysis relies heavily on the organization's ability to successfully convert tacit knowledge into explicit or transferable forms in a timely manner, which then can be shared across the business to contribute to its longer-term strategic direction. Figure 4.1 presents a matrix to illustrate group and individual sources of tacit or explicit knowledge. For the majority of organizations knowledge management has followed a two-fold approach of, first, organizing existing information and data and, second,

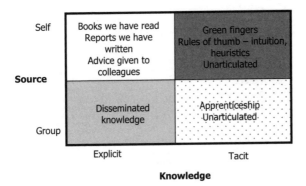

Figure 4.1 Knowledge type and source.
(From *Embracing Knowledge Management: The Impact on Organizational and Personal Performance*. S.A. Burtonshaw-Gunn and M.G. Salameh, 2008a, ICAFI University Press.)

facilitating the creation and development of new knowledge.

Looking at Figure 4.2 it is proposed that knowledge management is synergistic and not merely a collection of objective facts or "data" which can be presented without any judgement. Such facts only become converted into useful information after they are categorized, analysed, summarized and placed in context. In turn, such "information" provides a basis on which to make comparisons, assess consequences, establish connections, engage in a dialogue and form a basis on which to make business decisions. The addition of wisdom gained through experience, judgement, intuition and values offers benefits when used in combination with information in providing

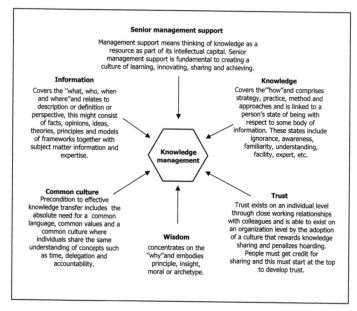

Figure 4.2 Model of knowledge management.
(From Knowledge management: a tool for gaining competitive advantage through intellectual capital development. S.A. Burtonshaw-Gunn, *Professional Consultancy Magazine*, 2006, reproduced with permission.)

a richer knowledge management system and indeed a sustainable performance advantage to the organization.

While the eminent Greek philosopher Aristotle considered "knowledge" as the driver of economic progress and the basis of power, today's organizations can regard knowledge management as a business activity with two primary objectives. The first of which is treating the knowledge component of an organization as an important aspect of business; this asset can be reflected in its strategy, policy and practices that can be cascaded to all levels of the organization. This first objective can be satisfied by information management, which typically covers storage of material, data, information, its recording and filing accessibility often with a technology focus and use of software tools that assume that the information can be standardized and automated. The second objective is to recognize and form a direct connection between an organization's intellectual assets and its business results; this can encompass identifying and mapping intellectual value within the organization, generating new knowledge, making corporate information accessible, sharing "best practice" and employing technology that can facilitate such development. These two objectives can provide the organization with a competitive advantage and provide a focus on work practice and culture while adding value to context by filtering, synthesizing and interpretation. However, the value of the second objective is not without a cost in terms of the often considerable effort it requires for its ongoing input and the encouragement for knowledge sharing and exchange. Indeed, to maximize the investment needed to establish an organizational approach to knowledge management, three key cultural/behavioural factors are proposed: senior management support, common culture and trust. These three elements are also shown in Figure 4.3 and need to be addressed not in a prosaic, mechanical or process way but should be wholeheartedly embraced and valued.

Figure 4.3   Elements of corporate culture.
(From *The Essential Management Toolbox: Tools, Models and Notes for Managers and Consultants.* S.A. Burtonshaw-Gunn, 2008, reproduced with permission.)

Within the knowledge-driven economy, the speed of change with which organizations are expected to respond has meant greater rewards such as competitive advantage or class-leading financial performance for those organizations which can develop an organizational culture that encourages, values and visibly rewards knowledge sharing.

This may be achieved, or encouraged, by breaking down the "silos" which often exist within more traditional business environments and incorporating knowledge as a key element of individual and team performance evaluation. Knowledge management may be undertaken as part of a change management programme.

As with many aspects of growth and development of corporate organizations it is the ability with which they can engage and motivate people to transfer their experiential learning and ideas to a wider community to harness greater value from such knowledge that is of major importance. This especially applies to the effect that behavioural and motivational factors have on the openness of the process and receptivity of participants. This is not a new phenomenon as there are numerous examples of culture-based learning as an established practice for professional services organizations such as those within business consulting and legal practices, for example. Developing this concept from a knowledge management perspective will require the nurturing of behaviours which support the business on a number of levels and may also result in a sense of well being among stakeholders – while helping to undo deep-seated perceptions that sharing knowledge is associated with losing personal ownership or control. Clearly, this type of culture needs a critical mass of individuals who recognize that their own knowledge and experience are precious assets, and when deployed to add value to the business will be reciprocated by the business through either financial or non-financial rewards. The model shown as Figure 4.3 covers elements of corporate culture and illustrates how both employee and employer behaviour, values and culture play a joint role in converting the organization's desired performance targets into meeting and supporting longer-term strategic objectives.

Having mentioned reward for knowledge, the challenge for organizations is not just about the most appropriate way to incentivize knowledge-sharing but also having an appreciation of the behavioural roadblocks that exist in traditional hierarchical cultures and often serve to inhibit the desired free and open exchange. Once the obstacles or resistors are identified and understood they can be addressed in a manner which enables people to contribute and feel more involved – most importantly, this can also increase their sense of emotional attachment to the business's values, products and services. Unfortunately, for many global corporate organizations the resisting forces are often too strong because of established hidden norms and legacy behaviours, where such restrictive attitudes only serve to reinforce primarily a fear of a loss of control. Such typical attitudes and behaviours will be recognizable to readers in the following examples:

- The existence of organizational "silos"; fostering a "them and us" mentality.
- Failing to recognize or even choosing to ignore subtle changes in market dynamics until it's too late.

- Placing more emphasis on current tasks and thus encouraging short-termism.
- Failing to adopt the appropriate feedback mechanisms to manage and review organizational learning.
- Allowing the business to be constrained by internal politics.
- Losing transparency through the growth of a blame culture, rather than learning from mistakes.

In considering knowledge from an individual perspective, many readers will know the famous quotation of the English lawyer and philosopher Francis Bacon that "Knowledge is power"; however, the 19th century American Senator Thomas W. Palmer suggested that more importantly: "Action is power; and its highest manifestation is when it is directed by knowledge". Although it has been over 100 years since Palmer's comment, the power of knowledge is perhaps even more important as a modern-day organizational tool in providing informed decisions on which to take action and contribute to business success. Equally successfully, managing performance has always relied on being equipped with the right knowledge, at the right time and in the right place in order to have the confidence to deal effectively with a wide range of personal performance issues that individuals may encounter within the workplace. Although earlier discussion centred on organizations setting the context and expectations for individual performance, it is the enabling effect knowledge management can have on an individual's willingness to take responsibility and address personal performance issues which is particularly valuable to key business decision makers.

By encouraging alignment of certain external talents or activities relating to an organization's employee population through conscious inclusion in a knowledge management strategy, huge additional experiential learning and knowledge sharing opportunities can be harnessed (such as personal sporting, academic or other voluntary interests). By promoting such a cultural change, employees can better connect to the business's markets, products and services; and by making this greater emotional investment can improve their individual performance by identifying areas of alignment between their personal beliefs and values, and those of the employer.

PEOPLE AND KNOWLEDGE MANAGEMENT

Clearly, there are a number of opportunities where an organization can connect with employees to realize such reporting performance benefits – probably the most obvious and certainly one of the most powerful in evolving individual performance and organizational learning is through "networking". Since the industrial age, individuals have benefited from the sharing of ideas and gaining new knowledge through membership of professional clubs

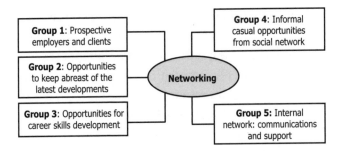

Figure 4.4 Networking as part of knowledge exchange. (From *The Essential Management Toolbox: Tools, Models and Notes for Managers and Consultants*. S.A. Burtonshaw-Gunn, 2008, reproduced with permission.)

and learned societies, allowing members to meet new people and explore common interests. In today's professional work world, individuals often have to select which groups or events to attend which will facilitate networking to their best advantage. These opportunities typically cover one of five main types of networking groups with each offering different benefits (see Figure 4.4).

- Some groups provide opportunities to interact with prospective employers and clients; and smaller businesses are encouraged to share experiences and ideas to improve in-house knowledge.
- Some groups enable their members to keep abreast of the latest developments in their field, such as technical products or managerial processes. These features are typical of many professional institutes' local branch meetings and special interest groups.

- Some networking groups provide opportunities for career skills development that will enable attendees to learn more about self-marketing, interviewing and making a successful transition. An example of this is a university alumni association.

- In addition to these formal networking groups is the use of a more casual network such as family and friends; local school contacts through children; patrons of the arts or charity groups.

- Finally, internal company networks can also be used to provide opportunities for idea exchange and support for implementation of new methods, processes or products.

Although some people profess to have access to a large business network, for the vast majority of these this relationship is passive and can be compared to collecting information and measuring metrics which nobody is interested in and as such is widely mistakenly considered as a de facto safety net. While there is a practical restriction on the amount of people any individual can know, the interaction with groups offers a linkage to others using networking and if carefully executed can create an opportunity to accelerate learning through a more active exchange of knowledge. Indeed, as each network node is connected to another network though people, Malcolm Gladwell's popular book *The Tipping Point* (2000) proposed what is now a widely accepted phenomenon that "six degrees of separation" allows a connection between any small group of people to the rest of the work. While it may be a powerful concept, the link strength comes from the role that individuals play in their own local networks and not by any group trying to organize itself through links to other networks in support of the six degrees of separation concept – a good example of quality rather than quantity perhaps. However, the benefit of networking is only fully realized where an individual is known and trusted by the group and, also importantly, where members feel comfortable to make the next connection with their other networks with which they have a trusted relationship. Without the attribute of developed trust and acceptance, the relationship with another network is likely to fail as the linkage will be immature and possibly regarded as superficial by the network members. Therefore for personal networking to provide real added value it needs to be carefully managed and continually rationalized otherwise individuals run the risk of hoarding far too many contacts which are never active and are incapable of satisfying future knowledge demands. Networking is a prime example of a common management tool with the potential to deliver greater individual and business performance by feeding directly into a corporate knowledge management strategy and contributing to increased business and individual awareness of changes in market dynamics, technological advances or even legislative impacts.

Considering knowledge management from a corporate stance, it is fair to say that many organizations have experienced roadblocks to the adoption of formal knowledge management activities, some of which were discussed earlier. As marketplaces are increasingly competitive and the rate of innovation is rising, there is a need to manage growing complexity as even small companies widen their influence by looking at international supply chain management to gain a competitive advantage, as can be seen by the increase of subcontract or manufacturing work undertaken in India and more recently in China. Fundamentally, integration of an organization's people supported by the right corporate culture allows technology to capture and manage raw data and information at an unprecedented rate, while its interpretation and application creates knowledge which may be valued as "intellectual capital" on its balance sheet. This should in itself provide the motivation to seek to remove the obstacles and make better use of the organization's own intellectual assets.

In developing and implementing a knowledge management strategy, it is imperative that it is fully aligned to the business strategy and uses business processes as key enablers in driving value. The benefits of carefully identifying and mapping current and future knowledge requirements and capabilities necessary to satisfy downstream business aspirations are threefold:

1. That those tacit and explicit knowledge requirements satisfy stakeholder expectations.
2. That an explicit and logical linkage is created between knowledge management and business strategies which helps manage resistance to change by making it more

difficult for people to avoid implementing any identified organizational changes.

3. And that it ensures business critical knowledge is prominent and thus more easily managed to yield significant benefits.

At this point, it is important to emphasize that any organization should also ensure that appropriate governance exists, to protect both the employee and the business – especially when considering the interaction between specialized knowledge and scarce skills.

With competitive pressures on businesses which may include downsizing and undertaking major corporate change in the organization's strategic direction, it is easy for valuable tacit knowledge, as a feature of everyday corporate life, to be lost forever. Of course, while there are normally advantages in such organizational changes there is also a risk that these will be undermined by corporate amnesia witnessed by examples across all businesses by spending hours on issues that previously took minutes. The loss of staff and valuable knowledge not only arises from the organization's actions but also with increased "knowledge worker" mobility. This consequence supports the words of the Spanish-born philosopher Jorge de Santayana y Borrás, that: "those who cannot remember the past are condemned to repeat it".

For maximum added value and improved business performance there will need to be an effective process to bring both corporate and individual approaches of knowledge management together. This could be done by taking advantage of existing networks and connections across departments or even the business footprint as a whole. In conjunction with these existing networks there will be a need to create new ones by process mapping (see also Chapter 1) the information flow and linkages, capturing areas where the organizational processes can be improved from the tacit knowledge held by individuals and translating that into specific process improvements – which in turn contribute to both organizational and individual performance and the increased value of both parties. The true winners in realizing the aspirations of the knowledge company will be those businesses who create new and innovative business opportunities by integrating their own capabilities and imagination, with those of the knowledge management disciplines discussed.

This chapter has explored the subject of knowledge management and its links to both organization and personal performance, looking at knowledge management from an individual performance perspective. In view of this, the concept of networking should be regarded as a valuable performance tool and be considered as an essential exercise in "personal branding" and the practical deployment of knowledge management adding to the individual's profile, credibility and consequently value. As a final point, networking should not be considered in isolation of other essential management tools, which are equally capable of enhancing individual and corporate performance through knowledge management.

CHAPTER 5

ORGANIZATIONAL DEVELOPMENT AND PERFORMANCE THROUGH COLLABORATIVE WORKING

DEVELOPMENTS IN COLLABORATIVE WORKING

With greater realization of a global economy, a number of organizations are unable to compete using their own resources and have to look for alternatives to gain a competitive advantage. For many companies, both products and services have increased in their complexity and value, therefore prosecuting new business opportunities often involves accepting greater levels of risk. The inevitable consequence of such competitive pressures is to pursue high-risk business winning opportunities by the formation of partnerships, especially when such circumstances are surrounded by high levels of uncertainty. This feature is not new as over 10 years ago Harvard University Professor Rosabeth Moss Kanter suggested that alliances between companies are a fact of life in business and that: "whatever the duration and objectives of the business alliances, being a good partner has become a key corporate asset" (source: *Harvard Business Review*, July–August 1994).

This alliance feature she later terms as a "collaborative advantage" for those companies who have developed the ability to create and sustain collaboration – resulting in a significant advantage over their competitors. For large organizations in particular, the attraction may be to form a strategic alliance or joint venture providing organizational performance advantages to both parties through the development and realization of business synergy. One form of strategic alliance, usually resulting in the formation of a new company, is a merger between two willing organizations which are usually developed from resource constraints among one or several of the cooperating entities. Typically, these alliances occur when funding is needed to capitalize a company's technological opportunity or that they are formed in order to reduce barriers to market entry; the latter is often synonymous with exploring new international markets. It should be noted that this type of alliance is very formal and should only be considered when the parties concerned have a good working knowledge of each other, have some cultural synergies, and are prepared to give the new organization their full commitment both financially and managerially.

An alternative approach is for organizations to develop capabilities to be able to meet the requirements of current and future customers, and instead of forming a joint venture, benefits may come from closer working within their respective supplier base. This supply chain approach prompts a series of cost and quality improvements which can contribute to the creation of more satisfied customers and hence increase the opportunities for repeat business. Such relationships are also seen in the much publicized Japanese "Keirutu" financial and industrial groups in which cross-ownership networks contractually tie buyers and suppliers together. Indeed, supply chain management itself has seen a significant growth over the last decade resulting in recognition of its strategic importance and the competitive advantage that it can offer. The range of collaborative options is shown in Figure 5.1.

The pressure to pursue collaborative working as a key source of collaborative advantage can be traced back to the different historical stages of the concept of "outsourcing" as we know it today. As the market for outsourced services has matured so the requirement to seek more innovative operational philosophies has given credence to

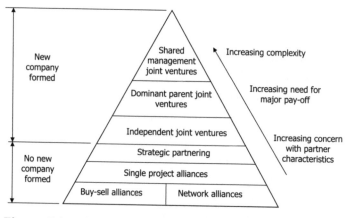

Figure 5.1   The range of collaborative working options.

adopting partnering as a key corporate strategy in increasing profitability and additional shareholder value. Therefore to fully understand the performance benefits of partnering shown in Figure 5.1 it is useful first to consider the historical market developments in outsourcing. Within what are termed the first generation arrangements between customers and suppliers in the early 1990s the relationships which existed then allowed typical profit margins in excess of 20% to be gained as a result of using outsourced resources. Many of these arrangements focused heavily on the removal of a problem for a customer and were grounded in the provision of safe and fairly low-risk quality solutions. However, new entrants through either start-up or diversifying organizations began to flood in to what appeared to be a lucrative market, presenting low barriers to entry and both attractive and accessible profit levels. At this point the need to collaborate as an essential element of business performance was only partially appreciated.

The growth in the outsourcing market was so rapid that by the mid-1990s, the intense competition in this provision gave rise to second generation arrangements which centred on cost-driven solutions; in the case of the UK government this promoted a move away from awarding traditional cost-plus contracts towards the use of fixed-price contracts. These second generation arrangements were so heavily weighted towards cost reduction that they were characterized by significant failures and a resulting rethink with the emergence of collaboration among suppliers, particularly new entrants through mergers, acquisitions and external management buy-outs (MBOs). Once again, this changed the relationship and balance between customers and suppliers – especially with respect to customer's performance expectations and their influence on competitive pressure within the global supply chain. This change in emphasis also became the catalyst for many corporate organizations, in the race for sustainability of profit margins and business growth, to consider collaborative partnering as a new source of competitive advantage, particularly those in manufacturing. By the late 1990s, third generation deals were heavily reliant on customer and supplier working in partnership, with the relationship being predicated on adding value and ensuring that this was demonstrable through transparent performance metrics, comparators and service level agreements (SLAs). This change is best evidenced by the paradigm shift within *inter alia* the defence, health, transport and education sectors where major procurement purchases were made through the Private Finance Initiative (PFI) funding mechanism.

SUPPLIER/CUSTOMER PARTNERING CONSIDERATIONS

The fundamental premise upon which any partnering collaboration should be entered into is to obtain the best long-term value for the organizations concerned. It is at this point that the primary difference between the public and private sector is at its most visible. Within public sector organizations, partner selection has to be conducted in a fully transparent manner; consequently, this is delivered through competition and evaluation of competing proposals – with an emphasis on selecting partners through an open process. At the core of this process of partner selection is the requirement of potential partners to provide metrics which demonstrate value for money (VfM) processes, practices and solutions; these need to outperform what is possible from a normal contractual arrangement for the same product, asset or service when delivered in a traditional customer–supplier procurement relationship.

In the private sector, although the ethical and governance-related aspirations of the public sector are still core elements in the partnership selection process, there is generally a greater emphasis on selecting a partner on the basis of entrepreneurial or financial characteristics which either increase market accessibility and addressability or which deny the competition the ability to respond with the same reach and flexibility. Clearly, this must be within the boundaries set by applicable anti-trust and fair competition legislation appropriate to the operating environment. However, a partnership in the private sector still needs to be able to withstand a high level of scrutiny by all commercial stakeholders and be able to demonstrate increased shareholder value. For both sectors there are a number of common denominators which need to be considered when selecting a partner for any longer-term commercial relationship, future alliance or partnering arrangement such as:

- Economic health and financial stability.
- Technical capability and capacity.
- Demonstrable and traceable past performance.

Further investigation and due diligence may focus on a deeper understanding of a potential partner's expectations, commitment and vision of the future synergies to be gained, evidenced through aspects of business performance related to:

- The complementary nature of short- and long-term business objectives.
- An integrated approach to business planning which does not conflict and allows for incentivization.

- The financial strength and innovative finance mechanisms.
- Existence of a risk management capability together with a process capable of sharing risk.
- Competency of management processes and an appropriate level of governance.
- The type of organizational culture (see also Figure 4.3) and level of empowerment (see also Figure 3.9).

In essence, for partnering to have a realistic chance of success, appropriate time and effort needs to be invested at the evaluation stage to ensure that an effective balance will exist during the contract life between the performance expectations to deliver VfM and the behaviours necessary to grow and sustain the relationship through partnering cooperation. While these particular strategies realize many of their predicted benefits they are also open to criticism as being typically limited to one-off solutions. An alternative approach using continuous improvement may result from the delivery of goods and services using strategic partnering with the key objectives of minimizing cost exposure, maximizing product, asset and service development, and ultimately delivering a competitive performance advantage. Additionally, a more tactical alliance may be sought in response to an organizational crisis, to strengthen a negotiating position or to increase purchasing power – where the intention of such tactical partnering is to target a particular business operational need and hence contribute to organizational performance.

However, the aspiration in any type of sustained collaborative relationship must be to coexist within a holistic partnership which continually identifies new areas of collaboration and draws on the strengths and successes of the individual partners, as well as the inevitable lessons learnt from the relationship undertaking. By actively cultivating such a relationship, opportunities may exist to redefine markets through innovation creating diversification; penetrate existing markets through service integration; and attracting the talent necessary to continually innovate and evolve commercial sustainability. Taking a more holistic approach to collaborative working has forced customers and suppliers (see Figure 5.2) to rely on their business

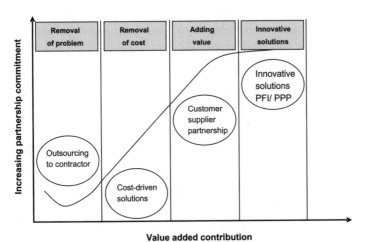

Figure 5.2 Business expectations of partnering.
(From *Harnessing Competitive Advantage through Tactical and Strategic Partnering*. S.A. Burtonshaw-Gunn and M.G. Salameh, ICAFI University Press, 2008b.)

partnerships as a vehicle for innovation. This performance opportunity is not just limited to the public sector partnering with the private sector, but all manner of consolidation between private sector organizations in a proactive drive to create innovative solutions, increase their activity in wider markets and benefit from complementary skills to deliver or receive higher levels of service and thus generate a competitive advantage.

Clearly, partnerships structured around a long-term commitment to provide through-life support of a product, service or asset require an even more diligent commitment to transparency, both in striving to continuously improve performance and for the longevity of the relationship beyond contract completion. Consequently, another key characteristic of any successful partnering arrangement is the ability for either party to have an exit strategy which accounts for commercial, operational and customer service-related commitments made during the contract life. These may include:

- The transfer of assets between partner and supplier (new operator).
- A commitment to any unfinished work.
- The ownership of joint intellectual property rights (IPR) in relation to any research, design and product development.
- Any investment decisions made in the latter stages of any partnering agreement leaving insufficient time to recover costs.

- The anticipated cost savings and performance improvements committed to through cooperation at key transition stages.

It is important to re-emphasize the point that partnering is essentially the development of new, innovative and more cooperative working relationships to increase business performance from problem solving and agreed common goals. With the exception of a very few cases when looking at supply chain management, it is the customer organization that takes the initiative in expressing an interest in partnering as a way to develop a strategic competitive advantage. This relationship may be formed with either new suppliers or, more commonly, with selected members of its existing supplier base. Moving to a longer-term partnering relationship will often allow the client organization to reduce the total number of suppliers it uses as future work can be awarded to its "new" partner rather than be competitively tendered. This results in savings of time, effort and the cost of managing a tender assessment process.

Looking closer at this type of relationship, partnering can be applied to one-off schemes (commonly referred to as "project partnering"), or can be ongoing over a series of developments (often called "strategic partnering") intended to govern a long-term relationship based on an agreed trading formula. An obvious partnering relationship is worthy of consideration when a mutual dependency between suppliers and customers occurs as

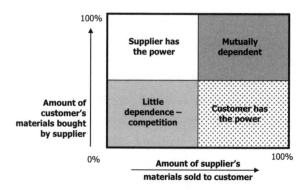

Figure 5.3 Trading between supplier and customer affecting importance of relationship development.
(From *The Essential Management Toolbox: Tools, Models and Notes for Managers and Consultants*. S.A. Burtonshaw-Gunn, 2008, reproduced with permission.)

shown in Figure 5.3. Conversely, where there is little or no dependence between suppliers and customers due to market size or the number of suppliers, there is rarely an advantage in committing resources in the development of a closer partnering relationship. There is much advice regarding the care that has to be taken to ensure that through partnering arrangements a legally binding agreement between the participants is not created which would require additional legal considerations of both a statutory and regulatory type.

Central to any successful partnering relationship is the willing involvement of all parties and the belief that together they will realize significant benefits above and beyond what is normally achievable within the boundaries of a standard provider–supplier contractual commitment. This development is often a natural step arising from an established existing relationship between companies that have previous successful experience of cooperation. However, for such benefits to be possible requires openness, honesty and above all a desire for continuous vigilance by all parties to identify further areas for development and growth within the value chain of the business arrangement. Such congruence allows the partnering relationship to take advantage of joint exploitation of market opportunities or third party revenue streams previously out of reach of each individual organization. Given that openness and trust are pivotal characteristics for any project or strategic partnership to be successful then consideration should be given to the other factors synonymous with developing a valuable partnering relationship. In many cases these characteristics can be grouped into five key areas as detailed below.

1. **Legal implications of partnering:** The legal implications of partnering need to be recognized and fully considered by companies prior to embarking on such a relationship. In general, partnerships and joint ventures share a number of features, although under English law going back to the Partnership Act of 1890, "partnership" has a specific meaning and there is a risk of unintentionally creating a legally binding relationship where none was intended. If true partnerships or joint ventures are created then there are

often taxation implications with tax assessments being undertaken on the partnership as a whole. This is more applicable to what can be termed as "horizontal partnerships" which cover partnering arrangements between similar suppliers, rather than "vertical partnerships" formed between suppliers and their end users or customers. From a European Union perspective, partnering will always be unlawful if its effect is to discriminate against undertakings on national grounds, or breach the fundamental freedoms of movement of goods, services, workers and capital. Even if a partnering arrangement does not affect trade between EU member states, it may still be void, punishable by fine or liable in damages under English law if the agreement imposes restrictions on the price and supply of goods. As such, care has to be taken in the establishment of a collaborative partnership to prevent the legal formation of a true partnership agreement as covered by such legislation, as their dissolution is often a long and complex issue.

2. **Contractual considerations and dispute resolution:** While the desire to reduce adversarial situations is one of the factors that attract commercial organizations to partnering, occasionally a problem between the parties may be so acute that its resolution requires attention by a more formal and structured process, but without damaging the parties' existing and future business relationships. The resolution of disputes is there-

fore an important issue and seen by many to be one of the cornerstones of collaborative partnering. Such resolution is not just to achieve a short-term settlement; more important is the fact that both parties will have invested considerable time and effort in establishing and developing a working relationship designed to operate over many years. On this basis, it is suggested that while disputes may arise and need to be dealt with, the management of the process may destroy the partnering relationship if either side believes that the other has reverted to contractual remediation without first exhausting an agreed collaborative settlement process.

3. **Personnel competency:** One of the most important aspects of any successful business venture is that of people as discussed in Chapter 3; however, this is particularly so for those working in a partnering relationship. In this circumstance, the people involved in the partnership arrangement must be the right quality in terms of technical skills, experience, attitude and competence together with a disposition towards the partnering philosophy. If these qualities are missing, or there are certain people not committed to the concept of partnering, then the relationship is more likely to fail. Thus, the selection of suitable staff to implement and develop a relationship is crucial to the success of the partnering process. To this end, both organizations involved will often need to consider the relative merits

of their own staff and decide how well each is able to contribute to working in a collaborative arrangement. The members of staff to be considered most carefully are those that make up the management team, as it is this group who have the largest influence on the relationship. Indeed, if any of these managers are not committed or exhibit the wrong behaviours, then the relationship is unlikely to be successful. For any organization, partnering for the first time the selection of suitable staff may have to take place during the actual partnering process although any personnel changes may inhibit initial progress of the relationship until the right team with the right attributes has been found to make the arrangement work.

4. **Strategic commitment to partnering:** The key factor is that the staff from two (or more) organizations have agreed to work together by having identified common aims and objectives with the belief that such an arrangement can be mutually beneficial. Some organizations may wish to enter a formal binding partnering arrangement, for example where such an arrangement is particularly appropriate for a long-term strategic relationship and in this situation the agreement between the parties, often called a framework agreement, will regulate the relationship and deal with management procedures applicable to long-term, multi-project work. If there exists the necessary level of strategic commitment to the partnering relationship then even a new organizational culture

can be embedded to embrace new technologies and processes at an early enough stage to provide a competitive performance advantage.

5. **Selection of partner:** While most successful partnerships tend to be developed from existing relationships, prospective partners need to be carefully selected with an emphasis on the compatibility of outlook and systems, and the empathy of key personnel. This is necessary as partnering companies need to understand not only their own needs but also those of their new partner. Initially, the selection should evaluate each potential partner in terms of their strategic goals, their resources and the nature of their corporate culture before committing to a closer, "intimate" business relationship. Those companies with partnering experience believe that a shared vision of strategic goals between partners is essential for success and should be founded on a "win–win" basis. Assuming that the organizations involved appear to have reasonably compatible cultures, and are willing to work at dealing with differences, then there are likely to be benefits to both organizations in this level of collaboration.

Looking at partnering in practice the selection of a partnering organization is an important task and should demand an understanding of the requirements of a partnering philosophy; however, the decision and selection of partners is more of a two-way process than may be initially thought. While the client may wish to select a contractor with partnering experience, quality standards, a good safety record, a track record of project performance, resources and a sound financial standing, those suppliers with such experience of partnering will be looking to enter a relationship with an "educated client".

Investing time on the partner selection is crucial to create a collaborative advantage which can realize significant and often tangible benefits:

- The end customers'/users' expectations of service levels, customer experience and performance are continually exceeded.
- The incentive to innovate through multi-skilled integration or consortial approach is far more consistent.
- Greater confidence and certainty exists around the accuracy of future performance delivery standards through jointly owned service level agreements.
- Risk is managed and rewarded more appropriately; consequently anticipated costs and budgets are better understood.
- Long-term perspectives are possible and thus whole-life efficiencies can be accounted for in tactical/operational objectives.
- Reduced lead times to delivery of a product or service, which features increasing levels of quality, can grow market strength and dominance.

• More intricate knowledge management and understanding of the market through partnership allows antic-
ipation of future trends and customers' latent needs.

The experience of many organizations has shown that
strategic partnering – like large-scale cultural change – is
unlikely to yield the full performance benefits in the
short term but these may be realized over a longer timeframe such as a five to 10 year period. On this basis, if
partnering is then considered as an alliance over the long
term there needs to be a significant organizational investment (both intellectual and developmental) made to help
foster and encourage a culture capable of embracing
significant change. Once a partnership reaches a more
mature state it is suggested that "benchmarking" can be
used to generate innovative ideas and process improvements, which will be advantageous to all parties and lead
to further increases in improved performance.

PARTNERING IN ACTION

This chapter has described a number of approaches and
how such relationships can be formed aimed at increasing
organizational performance. While there are many examples of a growing trend for suppliers and clients to embark
on project and strategic partnering relationships their
commitment to three key themes of mutual objectives,

problem resolution and continuous improvement is, in many cases, limited to establishing the mutual objectives with less emphasis on the other two themes. Indeed, with a general move by businesses to performance management hierarchies and careful monitoring of key performance indicators (KPIs), allied to continuous improvement, it is suggested that partnering supports this approach where performance can be witnessed in terms of quality, delivery, improved client satisfaction and greater flexibility.

The focus of the final model (Figure 5.5) – "Partnering in action" – relates to where the partnering philosophy

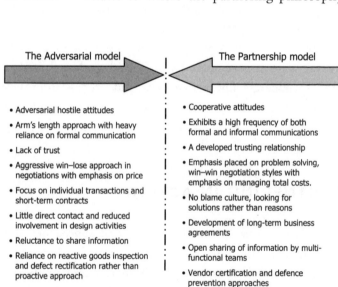

Figure 5.4 Relationship models.
(From *The Essential Management Toolbox: Tools, Models and Notes for Managers and Consultants.* S.A. Burtonshaw-Gunn, 2008, reproduced with permission.)

is being utilized and offers a representation of the issues likely to be encountered in the implementation and continuing management of the relationship. Each of the four primary components – project management, total quality management, supply chain management and human resource management – is represented by a quadrant together with the associated main subcomponents. The discussion of the subcomponents is focused towards the implications for closer collaborative working practices and relationships.

Human resource management: The strong emphasis on collaboration within the partnership suggests the need for effective human resource strategies and policies, designed to promote the appropriate attitudes and behavioural traits among those employees directly involved. As already discussed, the selection and training of the key senior staff concerned may be also critical to the partnering relationship's eventual success. As these requirements apply to both supplier and customer organizations there will often be merit in hosting joint staff development programmes such as team-building, project performance, problem resolution, etc.

Project management: Organizational structures and processes are important issues to be established at the outset to define the necessary roles and responsibilities and to strengthen the agreed communication channels. Within the partnering projects the project manager remains primarily responsible for delivering the project within the requirements of specification, time and budget, often regarded as the cornerstones of project management, together with achievement of client satisfaction. Establishing effective structures, processes, communication channels and relationships should discourage the adversarial approach and provide benefits in terms of efficiency (e.g. costs, workflow and flexibility) and effectiveness (e.g. meeting the client's needs and funding additional project requirements).

Total quality management: Partnering and total quality management may be viewed as highly complementary philosophies including the establishment of mutual objectives, the shared commitment towards continuous improvement and the need for mutually agreed measures of performance. As with partnering, the above features provide maximum opportunity over a longer timescale.

Supply chain management: The characteristics of the evolution towards strategic partnering relationships require a move away from selection on lowest tender price to consideration of whole lifecycle costs and value for money (VfM) as mentioned earlier. Important features of supply chain management include the initial selection of partners in the chain, building and developing effective relationships and agreeing arrangements for the nature of competition both within the partnership and with other suppliers and customers. In some industries, it is important that relationships are forged not only between the customer and the first-tier main contractor but also between the second-tier subcontractors and the prime contractor. Evidence from the manufacturing sector suggests that maximum benefit is gained by early and full involvement of all the key partners in the supply chain. Examples of early involvement are in design activities prior to ordering material for manufacturing or on–site construction works.

The other important feature of Figure 5.5 is the dynamic interaction between the subcomponents within

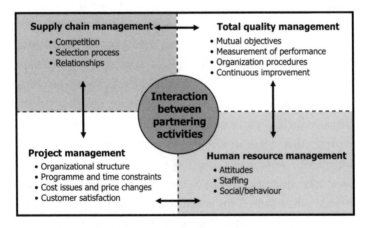

Figure 5.5 Partnering in action.
(From *People and Culture in Construction*. Professor S.A. Burtonshaw-Gunn and Professor R.L. Ritchie, 2007, reproduced with permission of Taylor and Francis.)

each of these four main groups and between the subcomponents in the other groups; for example, staff selection and appropriate attitudes (human resource management subcomponents) will influence simultaneously relationship development (a supply chain management subcomponent) and the effectiveness of continuous improvement (shown as a total quality management subcomponent).

With a strong emphasis being placed on a synergistic relationship, it should be remembered that each individual organization has a range of core competencies which make it unique and thus adopting a partnering arrangement should not result in a loss of organizational identity – especially where scarce skills and in-house competencies are concerned. It may be necessary to retain confidentiality in some of these key areas to ensure that the competitive edge results in a joint venture organization which is capable of harnessing such rivalry to mutual benefit and thus avoid the risk of complacency or inappropriate dominance. This also highlights an overarching characteristic common with all corporate business's decisions, which is particularly visible and applicable to partnering: that of senior management commitment to the objectives, aspirations and implementation of partnering as a key strategic business tool for providing a performance advantage. This is not to criticize the progress and benefits the partnering approach has made in practice but merely to advise that this is often not always the easy option initially perceived and will always require continual reinforcement of the partnership values illustrated in Figure 5.4. Finally, it should be appreciated that part-nering requires constant attention by senior, strategic champions within both organizations to maintain the momentum of the relationship and gain maximum per-formance benefits.

REFERENCES

Ahoy, C. (1999) Process mapping, facilities planning and management. *Facilities News Bulletin*, Iowa State University, USA.

Armstrong, M. (1994) *Performance Management Key Strategies and Practical Guidelines*. Kogan Page. ISBN 9780749445379.

Burtonshaw-Gunn, S.A. (2006) Knowledge management: a tool for gaining competitive advantage through intellectual capital development. *Professional Consultancy Magazine*, Issue 17, Institute of Management Consultants, UK.

Burtonshaw-Gunn, S.A. (2008) *The Essential Management Toolbox: Tools, Models and Notes for Managers and Consultants*. John Wiley and Sons, UK. ISBN 9780470518373.

Burtonshaw-Gunn, S.A. (2009) *Essential Tools for Management Consulting*. John Wiley and Sons, Ltd, UK. ISBN 9780470745939.

Burtonshaw-Gunn, S.A. (2010) *Essential Tools for Operations Management*. John Wiley and Sons, Ltd, UK. ISBN 9780470745922.

Burtonshaw-Gunn, S.A. and Davies E.M. (2008) *Guidelines for Successful Competency and Training Management*. Risktec Solutions Limited, Warrington, Cheshire UK, also see www.risktec.co.uk June 2008.

Burtonshaw-Gunn, S.A. and Ritchie, R.L. (2007) Developments in construction supply chain management, in *People and Culture in Construction* (A. Dainty, S. Green and B. Bagilhole, eds). Taylor and Francis, UK. ISBN 9780415348706.

Burtonshaw-Gunn, S.A. and Salameh, M.G. (2007a) *Change Management and Organizational Performance*. ICAFI University Press, Hyderabad, India. June 2007.

Burtonshaw-Gunn, S.A. and Salameh, M.G. (2007b) *The Role of Strategic Executive Development*. ICAFI University Press, Hyderabad, India. October 2007.

Burtonshaw-Gunn, S.A. and Salameh, M.G. (2008a) *Embracing Knowledge Management: The Impact on Organizational and Personal Performance*. ICAFI University Press, Hyderabad, India. June 2008.

Burtonshaw-Gunn, S.A. and Salameh, M.G. (2008b) *Harnessing Competitive Advantage through Tactical and Strategic Partnering*. ICAFI University Press, Hyderabad, India. March 2008.

Coulson-Thomas C. (1996) (ed.) *Business Process Re-engineering: Myth and Reality*. Kogan Page. ISBN 0749421096.

Gladwell, M. (2000) *The Tipping Point*. Little, Brown and Company, UK. ISBN 978-0316648523.

Hannagan, T. (2005) *Management Concepts and Practices*. 4th edition. Pearson Education.

Honey P. and Mumford A. (1986) *Using your Learning Styles*. Peter Honey Associates, Maidenhead, UK. ISBN 9780950844428.

Kanter, R.M. (1994) Collaborative advantage: the art of alliances. *Harvard Business Review*, July/ August 1994, 96–108.

Kübler-Ross E. (1969) *On Death and Dying*. Macmillan, New York. ISBN 9780415040150.

Nonaka, I. and Takeuchi, H. (1995) *The Knowledge-Creating Company: How Japanese Companies Create the Dynamics of Innovation*. Oxford University Press. ISBN 9780195092691.

Pendlebury, J., Grouard, B. and Meston, F. (1998) *The Ten Keys to Successful Change Management*. John Wiley and Sons, Ltd, UK. ISBN 9780471979302.

Philpott, L. and Sheppard, L. (1992) Managing for improved performance, in *Strategies for Human Resource Management* (M. Armstrong, ed.). Kogan Page.

Senge, P. (1994) *The Fifth Discipline: The Art and Practice of the Learning Organization*. Century Business/Doubleday. ISBN 9780385260954.

INDEX

Index compiled by Annette Musker